Reflection Questions

What attracted you to *Going First*? Why did you decide to buy it and work with this playbook?

_____

_____

_____

_____

How do you define "purpose"? What does "leading and living purposefully" mean to you?

_____

_____

_____

How do you think about purpose when it comes to your work? Your life? Is it a regular contemplation or a once-a-year crisis? Somewhere in between?

_____

_____

_____

Do you have a purpose statement (i.e., an explanation of why you do what you do in your work and/or life)? Even if it's not fully formed, jot something down here. No pressure, just write what comes. You'll be provided with guidance to refine it later on.

_____

_____

_____

My purpose is: _____

_____

_____

What's your #1 question about purposeful leadership?

_____

_____

_____

If you could change *one* thing in your life by reading *Going First* and working with this playbook, what would it be?

_____

_____

_____

How much time can you commit to working with this material each week? (If you're looking for a suggestion, we recommend one to two hours a week over ten weeks to give yourself time to integrate the content into real changes in your life.)

_____

_____

_____

Where will you do the work?

_____

_____

_____

_____

When will you do it?

_____

_____

_____

_____

How can you protect that time?

_____

_____

_____

_____

Are you ready to accept the mission? Why or why not?

_____

_____

_____

_____

_____

Part 1:

The Invitation

Your Invitation to Courage

This is your official invitation to join in the joyful endeavor of leading and living with purpose. In the first chapter of *Going First*, we looked at the foundation of what it means to have a purposeful life. A fundamental requirement for this process is courage, because making any change requires overcoming our fears. Courage is about being in touch with your heart. Although it may feel like jumping in front of a bullet, facing your fears with an open heart often reveals what you really care most about.

To overcome these fears, you must first identify what it is you're scared of. After all, we can't effectively address a challenge we don't understand. Build that clarity by revisiting the main points from this chapter and noting primary takeaways in your own words below. The questions in this section are designed to help identify your fears of leading purposefully—often masked as "the way things are" or other deeply held beliefs—and how you can start to overcome them.

Chapter 1 Notes

What does being a purposeful leader mean to you?

_____

_____

_____

_____

_____

_____

What does courage mean to you, and how does courage relate to creating change?

_____

_____

_____

_____

What are some of the risks of purpose discovery?

_____

_____

_____

_____

What's a simple path to courage?

_____

_____

_____

_____

Other Notes

_____

_____

_____

_____

_____

_____

Reflection Questions

What are you most afraid of when it comes to Going First? What are your main fears or hesitations about taking on this mission?

_____

_____

_____

How are you feeling about accepting this invitation? Does jumping into this work scare you? Why or why not?

_____

_____

_____

When have you taken courageous action in the past (no matter how small)? What helped you get over your fears and do it?

_____

_____

_____

When did you _not_ take an action that would've required courage? What held you back? How do you feel about that choice in retrospect? Is there anything you would've done differently?

_____

_____

_____

How does your body feel when you're being courageous?

_____

_____

_____

_____

_____

Circle your primary way of being when it comes to your style of thinking and working:

ANALYTICAL   EMPATH   ACTIVIST

Which fits you best at work? _____

Which fits you best in your personal life? _____

Which fits you best in your community? _____

According to your primary way of being noted above, what initial action can you adopt to support your Going First choices? Have you tried similar approaches in the past or learned other approaches that led you to courage? What were they?

_____

_____

_____

_____

CHAPTER 2:

Your Invitation to Purpose

In chapter 2, we proposed a rebrand of the term "purpose," from a vague, meaningless, and trendy concept to a fundamental aspect of successful ways of thinking, living, and working in this era. To jumpstart that rebrand, our focus in this chapter is to start somewhere with a small but concrete action that gives you some sense of fulfillment.

You'll start by reviewing what purpose is and what it isn't. Then you'll engage with some questions to get clearer about the notion of purpose as we're using it here. Finally, you'll craft your own (evolving) purpose statement. Don't worry—it's painless!

Chapter 2 Notes

What are some of the skepticisms you've heard about the idea of "purpose"?

_____

_____

_____

_____

What is purpose not?

_____

_____

_____

_____

How is purpose done right?

_____

_____

_____

_____

_____

Do you have a purpose statement yet? Why or why not?

_____

_____

_____

_____

_____

Other Notes

_____

_____

_____

_____

_____

_____

_____

_____

Reflection Questions

What's your current feeling or thinking about purpose? Has is changed from how you first viewed it before reading this chapter? If so, why?

_____

_____

_____

_____

_____

What's the reason you're most eager to get up in the morning, or at least, what was it today?

_____

_____

_____

_____

_____

When I say, "We get fulfillment from contributing to others' well-being. Understanding what will improve their well-being means closely examining their suffering, but it does not require _us_ to suffer," what's your response to this thought?

_____

_____

_____

_____

My Down and Dirty Purpose Statement

Having a loose, nonbinding draft of a purpose statement is a helpful premise for our pursuit to integrate purpose into all that we do. Recall the advice in the book to look for just that one eight-billionth of the world's problems that you're well-suited to contribute to; you don't have to do it all! Remember, this is an evolving process, not a binding statement about the next 40 years of your life. Perfect is the enemy of good, so just start somewhere!

Here are three simple steps for painlessly drafting a working purpose statement that you can use to organize your thinking about what impact you want to have:

Step 1:

Think about all the problems that are affecting the people you care about. What news stories make your heart beat faster? What frustrates or angers you most? What innovations or solutions inspire you? (Remember that you can look at these issues up close without suffering directly.)

_____

_____

_____

_____

Based on this quick brainstorm, pick one problem or perhaps an overarching one that includes a few that you thought of. What exactly is the change you want to contribute to that would address some element of that problem?

What: _____

_____

_____

_____

_____

Step 2:

Think about who (or what) you aim to serve by solving that problem and write it below. Please remove judgment at this stage. If you picture serving colleagues on your team, your family members, or your neighborhood, those are the right audiences for this version of your purpose statement. Remember that your actions don't have to be dramatic or lifesaving to be worthy pursuits. Indeed, it's often most realistic—and thus most impactful—to focus your efforts on those close to you, within your circle of influence.

Who:
_____
_____
_____
_____
_____

Step 3:

Think about how you're going to contribute to driving this change for these people. Again, I recognize that there are entire books and development programs dedicated to identifying your strengths. This is a shorthand version. What is it you do when you're at your best?

How:
_____
_____
_____
_____

And just like that, you've got the components for a purpose statement that follows this formula:

THE FORMULA

I want to change [what you want to see] for [who you want to serve]
by [the unique way you can contribute].

YOUR PURPOSE STATEMENT

_____

_____

_____

_____

_____

These words won't be etched on your tombstone or published on your LinkedIn headline, so avoid analysis paralysis and give yourself room to play. Live with this draft for a few weeks at least. Read it out loud to see if it feels authentic. Can you connect it to your daily agenda? And if not, is that because the statement isn't right or because your daily agenda needs to change?

Bonus Step

If you're on a roll and want a next step, ask others about their purpose. Once you've drafted your own purpose statement, it becomes easier to ask friends, family, social media, and coworkers about the problems they care about.

What to Bring to the Party

In chapter 3, we considered the traits we need to bring with us on our path of purposeful living. Specifically, we need to bring our authenticity, self-acceptance, self-awareness, willingness to change, tenacity, and purpose to the purpose party. Before getting deeper into each element, take some time to review what each means to you. Then use the follow-up questions to expand and build upon your understanding of the necessary preparation for a Purpose Party. You'll end with a motivating statement and a quick introduction to the ABCs of Purposeful Leadership.

Chapter 3 Notes

How do you think about authenticity? When are you authentic in your life? At work? When are you not able to be?

_____

_____

_____

_____

Think about a time when your actions caused a ripple effect. What happened? How did it make you feel?

_____

_____

_____

_____

What's one thing you'd be willing to change about yourself that would help you have the impact you seek?

_____

_____

_____

_____

How do think about tenacity? Have you ever been particularly tenacious about something? What was it? How did it make you feel?

_____

_____

_____

_____

What activities are you currently doing in your life that you could connect to a larger purpose, the way Jeff did with exercise and parenting?

_____

_____

_____

_____

Other Notes

_____

_____

_____

_____

_____

Authenticity

The complexity of the problems we're facing means that they'll only be solved if every single one of us contributes in our unique ways to our respective work and lives. We must lean deeply into our unique profiles and get clear about what we want to do and where, when, and with whom we want to do it.

If you were completely empowered to contribute to one problem in a way that perfectly fits your skills, interests, and realm of influence, what would that look like? Feel like?

Does your work feel authentic to you? Why or why not?

How could you be more authentic in your life and work?

Self-Acceptance

Purposeful leaders find ways to make their unique profiles create positive outcomes even when people or systems around them don't see that uniqueness as a strength. Taking the time to identify and refine exactly the ways you can contribute most powerfully will optimize the influence you have on the people and planet around you.

What unique quality or qualities have you learned to accept about yourself?

_____

_____

_____

_____

How has self-acceptance impacted your life and/or work?

_____

_____

_____

_____

_____

What's one element of your unique approach that you might've seen as a weakness or challenge that could actually work to your advantage, as Ward, Tanya, Nuno, and Sylvana experienced?

_____

_____

_____

_____

_____

Self-Awareness

Our childhood experiences shape the ways we contribute and the issues we care most about. In any role, we must be willing to first learn our own unique ways of working and then lead in a way that fits us best. As Ward pointed out in the book, "Self-awareness is the path to self-actualization, by helping us understand what actions to take."

What experiences from early in your life might influence the ways you're best positioned to contribute?

_____

_____

_____

What are the mental and physical routines, key skills, working styles, frustrations, and skill gaps that are necessary to do your best work?

_____

_____

_____

What activities have you always enjoyed?

_____

_____

_____

What issues have you always cared about?

_____

_____

_____

Willingness to Change

Reawakening our natural connection to purpose often requires doing new things, meeting new people, or engaging with the same people in new ways. To start Going First, you'll likely have to change some habits, resist tradition, question assumptions, and relearn a lot.

What changes have you made successfully in the past? Why were they successful? What motivations, strategies, and/or tactics worked for you?

_____

_____

_____

_____

_____

_____

_____

What changes would you like to make now but struggle with? What do you think the obstacles are? Is it a matter of time, effort, skill, fear, or other logistical constraints or emotions?

_____

_____

_____

_____

_____

_____

_____

Now that you know something you'd like to change and some reasons you might struggle to do so, try linking the change to your purpose by crafting a motivating statement like the one below. Keep this statement with you as a reminder to help you overcome the obstacles you foresee.

MOTIVATING STATEMENT FORMULA

I am motivated to be / do more [desired change]
so that [desired outcome for the people or planet around me].

YOUR MOTIVATING STATEMENT

_____

_____

_____

_____

_____

_____

Tenacity

Since working with purpose is a marathon, not a sprint, leading purposefully has its demands. So you must manage your energy. Start by recognizing what drains you and what replenishes you.

What habits or values have you managed to maintain despite pressure from family, friends, colleagues, or media? How have you held onto them?

_____

_____

_____

_____

_____

_____

_____

What habit or value are you struggling to maintain right now? How could you connect that value more closely to your purpose to motivate yourself to keep it up?

_____

_____

_____

_____

_____

_____

_____

Your Purpose as You Understand it Today

As you continue to define your purpose and refine your purpose statement, answer the following reflection questions:

What topics make your heart race or induce you to read all the way to the end of an article?

What kind of a world do you picture for your grandchildren, real or imagined?

What would you like to see change before you leave this earth?

What do you consider your responsibility is in being purposeful?

The ABCs of Purposeful Leadership

The ABCs of Purposeful Leadership are one of the foundations upon which the whole Purpose Party model is built. Continually reviewing them as you work your way through your purpose journey helps you stay grounded and motivated.

In the chart below, write your personal definition of each of the ABCs as they relate to purposeful leadership. Then, to help make them specifically relevant to you, identify an area of your life or work in which each element tends to matter most.

	MY PERSONAL DEFINITION	WHERE THIS MATTERS MOST IN MY LIFE
Awareness		
Belief		
Clarity, Confidence, Courage		
Dive In		
Evolve & Evaluate		

Cutting Down the Noise

Preparing the items we need for an impactful Purpose Party and remembering the ABCs of Purposeful Leadership is relatively straightforward. But straightforward doesn't mean easy. In a world where our reality seems to change on an hourly basis and the algorithms reinforce our current thinking by the second, it's not easy to be open to changing our ideas or behaviors. So developing some sort of mindfulness practice to access this level of reflection is actually step zero of living purposefully. Remember, mindfulness looks different for all of us. It might be meditation or knitting. It might be walking, running, or cuddling with a pet. It might be stargazing, doing yoga, skiing, or playing the drums. As long as it captures your full attention, it gets your brain where you need it!

In the chart below, list some ways you can "cut the noise" to be more mindful of your purpose journey.

ACTIVITY	WHEN/WHERE/HOW

Results, or Why You Want to Accept this Invitation

In chapter 4, we covered the benefits of leading and living with purpose. It isn't sustainable, much less energizing, to do "good work" as a moral obligation. But when we do "good" (and often hard) work because it aligns with our skills, passions, and needs—connects to our purpose—it's empowering for us and those around us. Recognizing the potential benefits of identifying the activities that feel purposeful for you can drive the change you want to see. Doing those activities is where you'll be at your best and create the most positive results for yourself, your teams, and the world around you. In other words, it's a win-win-win, which is a much more sustainable arrangement than doing something out of guilt or obligation.

Before digging deeper into the benefits of living and leading with purpose in three dimensions of output (Me, We, and World), review the overall benefits and record your thoughts. Then you'll apply these thoughts to the three dimensions and continue gaining clarity and confidence about accepting your invitation to the Purpose Party.

Chapter 4 Notes

What are the advantages of taking a long-term, interconnected, holistic view of success?

_____

_____

_____

_____

_____

Which benefits of leading with purpose are most appealing to you?

_____

_____

_____

_____

_____

_____

List the basic elements of your Me dimension.

_____

_____

_____

_____

_____

_____

List the basic elements of your We dimension.

_____

_____

_____

_____

_____

_____

List the basic elements of your World dimension.

Give an example of a time you've felt each of the two types of happiness.

Other Notes

Now that you've reviewed the basics, I invite you to reflect on how the benefits of leading purposefully affect the impacts *you* have in your Me, We, and World dimensions. Stay in a brainstorming frame of mind and consider "impact" broadly. There might be intellectual, physical, spiritual, emotional, financial, and/or energetic outcomes. Take a minute to complete the chart below. Describe what would happen in your Me, We, and World dimensions if you lived more in line with the latest version of your purpose statement you wrote in the last chapter.

For example, does (or could) a sense of purpose in your Me dimension impact your health and happiness? Your performance at work? Your ability to gain clarity? Does (or could) a sense of purpose in your We dimension impact your team's performance, your company's profits, your family life, or your community? How about in the World dimension? Does it (or could it) impact whether how much your business gives back? Is your business focused more on hedonia or eudaimonia? How much do you contribute to justice in the world?

To further guide you in filling out this chart, think (or write) about your answers to the following reflection questions:

Reflection Questions

How have you felt the power of purpose improve your mental or physical state, motivate you, enhance your performance in a personal pursuit or at work, or clarify your choices?

_____

_____

_____

_____

_____

_____

_____

How have you seen your team harness the power of purpose to get clear, aligned, and motivated? What was the purpose? How did it affect business outcomes? How about the team's wellbeing?

_____

_____

_____

_____

_____

_____

_____

_____

How have you seen purpose at work in another team or company, at home, or in a community setting? Identify the motivating purpose and outcomes for that group.

_____

_____

_____

_____

_____

_____

_____

_____

Does your business intentionally make choices that are good for people and the planet? If not, where do you see opportunities in which different choices could result in better results?

_____

_____

_____

_____

_____

_____

_____

_____

If you've been part of a charitable giving program at your company or the recipient of corporate gifts at a not-for-profit, what was great about it? What downsides or conflicts did you see or feel?

_____

_____

_____

_____

_____

_____

_____

_____

_____

	MIND Intellectual, strategic, or political wellbeing	**BODY** Physical health, financial security, and environmental wellness	**SPIRIT** Emotional, spiritual, cultural, and societal wellness
Me			
We			
World			

Part 2:

Leading Purposefully

CHAPTER 5:

The Spectrum of Impact

In part 2 of *Going First*, we began exploring the frameworks for leading purposefully, specifically the Spectrum of Impact™, the Spheres of Impact™, and the Impact Dashboard™. Here we're going to work with the Spectrum of Impact, which describes the full array of organizations that can—and should—create positive social and environmental impact.

The Spectrum of Impact helps address the misconception that doing good and making money are mutually exclusive. The breadth and depth of change we need to achieve a healthy and equitable world requires an all-hands-on-deck approach, and each sector has a different but critical role to play. This approach is an opportunity to get involved in the motivating and rewarding work of doing business that's good for the world.

Take some time to review how the four main types of organizations on the Spectrum are having impact. Then you'll consider your own interactions with each of these types of organizations.

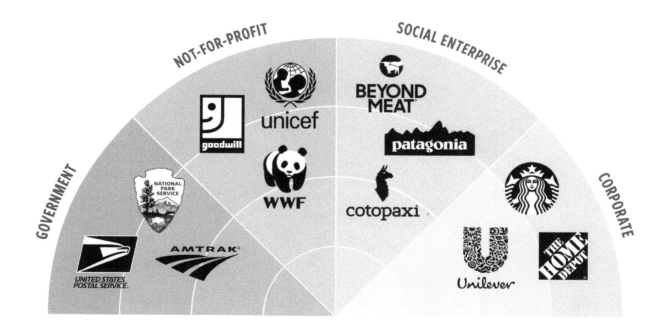

Chapter 5 Notes

How are government agencies positioned to make an impact? How and where do they struggle to have impact?

How are not-for-profits positioned to make an impact? How and where do they struggle to have impact?

How are Businesses for Good positioned to make an impact? How and where do they struggle to have impact?

How are corporations positioned to make an impact? How and where do they struggle to have impact?

The Spectrum of Impact

Now that you're more familiar with what companies do and how they choose to do it, take a moment to assess your own current Spectrum of Impact. In doing so, think or write about your answers to the following:

Government

How do you most often interact with the public sector? By voting? Donating to candidates? Serving on a local board or committee? Working for a government agency?

_____

_____

_____

_____

_____

_____

Not-for-Profit

How do you currently interact with not-for-profits? By donating money or supplies? Volunteering your time? Serving on a board? Working at a job with a not-for-profit?

_____

_____

_____

_____

_____

_____

Businesses for Good

How do you think or feel about the notion "business as a force for good"? What are some B Corp-certified companies or public benefit corporations you've heard about or had experience with?

_____

_____

_____

_____

How do you currently interact with Businesses for Good? By buying their products? Referring them to colleagues, friends, and family? Investing in them through the public markets or privately?

_____

_____

_____

_____

Corporate

How do you currently interact with private sector companies? Global corporations? Do you buy from them? Hold their stock? Are you in the 50 percent of the US workforce that has a job with a large (over 500 employees) for-profit company?

_____

_____

_____

_____

Considering your answers, rank how involved you are in each sector on a scale of 1–10, with 1 being minimal and 10 being very active. Note where and how you are currently making those investments.

	INVOLVEMENT RATING	ORGANIZATIONS YOU CURRENTLY INTERACT WITH	YOUR ROLE (investor, customer, employee, volunteer, fan, etc.)
Government			
Not-For-profit			
Businesses for Good			
Corporate			

From these reflections, what do you notice in terms of where you invest your time, attention, energy, and/or money overall? In what parts of the Spectrum would you like to increase, decrease, or change your interactions?

_____

_____

_____

_____

Government

How would you like to interact more with government institutions or find ways to achieve your desired outcomes that involve working with the public sector in some way?

_____

_____

_____

_____

Not-for-Profit

How would you like to interact more with not-for-profits or achieve your desired impact that involve working with them in some way?

_____

_____

_____

_____

Businesses for Good

How would you like to interact more with Businesses for Good or achieve your desired impact that involve working with them in some way?

_____

_____

_____

_____

_____

_____

LEARN MORE ABOUT CERTIFIED B CORPS

LEARN MORE ABOUT CONSCIOUS CAPITALISM

Corporate

How would you like to interact more or engage less with companies and corporations or achieve your desired outcomes that involve working with corporations in some way?

_____

_____

_____

_____

_____

Getting to Know the Impact Dashboard

In chapter 6, we began interacting with the Impact Dashboard, an interactive tool (game, really!) that helps you recognize the influence you're already having and where you could do more to have the impact you seek. You activate your purpose by choosing how to invest your resources of time, energy, attention, and money. Your Dashboard is intended to be drafted, revisited, and revised throughout your life.

But before mapping your efforts on the Dashboard, take some time to review what the Impact Dashboard is and how it can help you track your purpose journey. Then you'll narrow your focus to explore what specific investments feel engaging, exciting, or even joyful to you.

Chapter 6 Notes

What's your impression of the Impact Dashboard? Does it remind you of anything else?

_____

_____

_____

_____

_____

_____

_____

What's a good tempo for fully integrating your Dashboard into your life and work? How often and when do you plan to revisit it?

_____

_____

_____

_____

_____

How can you best prepare for working with your Impact Dashboard based on the basic elements described in the chapter? For example, do you need to practice more? Start enlisting accountability partners? Better align your activities?

_____

_____

_____

_____

_____

Other Notes

_____

_____

_____

_____

_____

_____

_____

_____

Elements of the Impact Dashboard

At the end of this playbook, you'll be guided in setting up a specific plan for living your Dashboard over time. For now, prepare yourself by focusing your reflection on four main ideas presented in this chapter by answering the following questions.

It's a Regular Practice

How do you foresee spending time with the Dashboard?

_____

_____

_____

_____

What do you need to help you stay on track with this plan?

_____

_____

_____

_____

How might your time and effort working with your Dashboard pay off?

_____

_____

_____

_____

What are your initial ideas about how you want to adjust your daily, weekly, monthly, or quarterly habits of purposeful leadership and reflection?

_____

_____

_____

_____

It's Stronger in Community

How can sharing your Dashboard with others help you on your purpose journey? How might it help them?

_____

_____

_____

_____

List three people with whom you can share your purpose work.

1. _____

2. _____

3. _____

List three ways you can share your purpose work with those people (or others).

1. _____

2. _____

3. _____

It Requires Both Care and Challenge

What's your reaction to Kelly Wendorf's Kanyini Care model?

_____

_____

_____

_____

_____

How have you experienced this kind of relationship or used its concepts in the past?

_____

_____

_____

_____

_____

How can you balance care and challenge in your purpose work, to yourself first, and then to others?

_____

_____

_____

_____

_____

It's about Aligning Activities, Not Adding Them

Being more purposeful is *not* just about adding to-dos to your plate. It can be powerful to *stop* doing things and/or adapt your current ways of doing things to be more aligned with your purpose. Maybe you just have to change how you frame them, who you do them with, or who you tell about the experience. By being intentional about the investments you make in each Sphere of Impact, you can use your time purposefully and, just as importantly, protect your time from other activities that don't serve your highest priorities.

What activities are you doing now that don't connect to the impact you want to have or represent your highest priorities, whether in the Me, We, or World dimension? Why do you do them? What would happen if you stopped doing them?

_____

_____

_____

_____

_____

_____

How can you free up your time, energy, attention, or money to do the things that are most aligned with the impact you want to have?

_____

_____

_____

_____

_____

_____

A Practical Approach to Tracking Your Impact

Tracking our habits is an essential element of making change. By tracking your habits, you'll start to see patterns emerge that look and feel like reasons for getting up in the morning. It's in this specificity about your actions that you can hold yourself accountable for having the influence you seek, track the learning when you get it right, and see when you need to course correct. Knowing that your Impact Dashboard is a living document that will, and should, evolve along with your evolving habits, it's important to practice with some available tools in preparation for engaging with and tracking your Dashboard work.

Take some time to explore my favorite habit trackers and apps at the link below to become familiar with how they can assist you in staying motivated and on track.

When you start diving deeply into each Sphere of Impact, you'll be working with my Weekly Purposeful Habit Tracker template, my Annual Planning Template, and my Impact Dashboard Excel Template. Take some time to review them now so that you're familiar and more comfortable with these tools when it comes time to use and apply them.

 CHECK OUT MY FAVORITE ACCOUNTABILITY TOOLS HERE!

www.inspiringcowgirl.com/tools

 DOWNLOAD MY TEMPLATES!

www.inspiringcowgirl.com/goingfirst

Diving in to Using the Dashboard

Now that you're familiar with the Impact Dashboard, it's time to dive in and practice the process you'll be following from here on to review each sphere in greater detail. In this chapter, we learned about Baseline Assessments and how they relate to the ABCs of Purposeful Leadership. We then zeroed in on how to use those assessments within each Sphere of Impact to identify the activities that really move the needle; in other words, those that have outsized payoffs that extend beyond yourself and impact the people and planet around you.

Before doing your own Baseline Assessment, take some time to review the basics of its five-step model. Later in this playbook, there is a guided process for applying the model to your own Dashboard to best align with your purpose and desired impact. For now, simply capture any immediate thoughts about Baseline Assessments and how they shape the path of your purpose journey.

Chapter 7 Notes

What's a Baseline Assessment and how can it inform your purpose journey?

_____

_____

_____

_____

_____

_____

How does *awareness* play a role in your purpose journey?

_____

_____

_____

_____

_____

_____

How does *belief* play a role in your purpose journey?

_____

_____

_____

_____

_____

_____

How do *clarity, confidence,* and *courage* play a role in your purpose journey?

_____

_____

_____

_____

_____

_____

How does *diving in* play a role in your purpose journey?

_____
_____
_____
_____
_____
_____

How do *evaluate* and *evolve* play a role in your purpose journey?

_____
_____
_____
_____
_____
_____

Other Notes

_____
_____
_____
_____
_____
_____

Your Baseline Assessment

Now that you've got the basics down, let's use the process for your own Baseline Assessment. You'll start with a simple brainstorm of how you've been spending your time in general before creating a plan for tracking and maintaining your purpose journey. You can use the questions on page 92 of *Going First* to help guide you.

Remember to balance care and challenge as you proceed through this work. Challenge yourself to learn, grow, and change. And also, have grace, realizing that it takes time and mistakes are inevitable. If you don't believe me, you can review the evolution of my Dashboard process in chapter 7 of the book. For further inspiration, you can also review the case studies presented there to remind yourself how Purpose Seekers Gabriela, David, and Lisa used their assessments to determine how and where they could best align their activities with their distinctive interests and needs.

To begin, start by getting into true brainstorming mode by doing a quick mini-mindfulness practice, such as taking a moment to breathe deeply or sit still with your eyes closed. There are no judgments in this process. All answers that come to mind are valid.

Now, write down what you spend your time doing. (You can use the downloadable Impact Dashboard Excel Template available via the QR code or on my website, or you can use the down and dirty chart on the next page.) Start with what you did today or yesterday. Pull out your calendar, if that's helpful, and go back through the last week, just jotting down a word or phrase to describe the things you spent your time doing. For now, ignore all but the first column.

When you're done with your initial brainstorm, review your list and add any important activities that are missing—maybe things that are less regular, such as a vacation, monthly massage, or quarterly catchup with a mentor. Don't forget to add sleep, a critical activity for wellness in the Self Sphere of Impact.

 DOWNLOAD THE IMPACT DASHBOARD EXCEL WORKSHEET AND OTHER TEMPLATES HERE!

www.inspiringcowgirl.com/goingfirst

ACTIVITY	TIME SPENT (HOURS PER WEEK)	SPHERE*	MORE, LESS, OR THE SAME

*Spheres: Self, Family and Friends, Job, Workplace, Community, Money

Estimate how many hours a week you spend on each activity and jot those numbers down in the second column. If you love this kind of stuff, go ahead and get really detailed about it (there's space in the Excel template if you're using that). And if the idea of counting hours gives you chills, don't worry; this is really just a quick, top-of-mind estimate.

For those less-than-weekly activities, include what they break down to on a weekly basis. There are 168 hours in a week (10,080 minutes, if that's the unit you use). So, for example, if your monthly hike with friends is a four-hour event door-to-door, put down one hour a week. If you spend 90 minutes with your mentor each quarter, it's about 0.1 hour a week. The idea is not to count your time to nanosecond-level accuracy but to get a rough idea of how much time you're spending on which activities. Do a quick check of how exhaustive your list is by adding up your time.

In the third column, assign each activity you listed to a sphere, either Self, Family and Friends, Job, Workplace, Community, or Money. It's okay if you don't yet know the specifics about each sphere; if you're uncertain about which sphere to put an activity in, trust your instinct and move on. This is just an initial brain dump. You can always recategorize or add activities as you continue learning more about each sphere. (You'll fill in the fourth column as you work through each sphere.)

And just like that, you're done with your Baseline Assessment! Save this list in whatever form you wrote it, because it's an important, foundational part of mapping your Dashboard in the chapters to come. As you think through each sphere in the coming chapters, you can look back and see if and how your at-a-glance assessment holds.

Reflection Questions

What did your Baseline Assessment tell you at a glance? How do you feel about it?

_____

_____

_____

_____

_____

Since evaluating and evolving is an essential step to make this process sustainable and meaningful, it's now worth planning ahead a bit so you'll be ready when you start your work in the first sphere.

What has worked for you to build new habits in the past? What hasn't worked?

_____

_____

_____

_____

What are your first and second choices to try: habit tracker app, an accountability buddy at work or home, a highly visible checklist, or gold stars. (Don't be surprised if these tools feel a bit juvenile or silly; we've got to work with our neurology, and these seemingly trivial tools work!)

_____

_____

_____

_____

What will you need on hand when you get to this point in each of the spheres? A downloaded app? Checklist? Gold stars?

_____

_____

_____

_____

When tracking your purpose journey, it's important to capture not only this type of quantitative data (how often did I do the thing) but also qualitative information (how did it make me feel and what effect did it have) about your new purposeful habit(s).

How will you record this qualitative information? A journal? Quarterly updates with yourself? Quiet reflection sessions?

_____

_____

_____

_____

What will you need on hand to do this, and how might you stay motivated?

_____

_____

_____

_____

In the book, each Purpose Seeker summarized their initial learnings in three sections: What I'm Doing, What I'm Not Doing, and Am I Doing Me?

Does this summary seem like it would be useful to you? Why or why not?

_____

_____

_____

_____

Are there other questions that would work better for you? What are they?

_____

_____

_____

_____

_____

_____

If this is useful to you, how will you record it?

_____

_____

_____

_____

_____

_____

How will you record your answers to those question and keep track of your progress?

_____

_____

_____

_____

_____

_____

Perilous Pitfalls to Leading Purposefully and How to Overcome Them

Now that you've done your Baseline Assessment, and before diving deep into each Sphere of Impact, it's important to recognize and understand the most common obstacles to leading and living with purpose. These are the perilous pitfalls that show up in the Me, We, and World dimensions, keeping us from improving our own well-being or that of other people and our planet. Since acknowledging a challenge is the first step to overcoming it, becoming familiar with these pitfalls and the problems they can lead to will help you overcome them when they show up.

In just a moment, you'll be evaluating how each pitfall affects you and your desired impact on the people and planet around you. First, take some time to review each pitfall, why it happens, and how you can overcome it.

Chapter 8 Notes

PITFALL	WHAT IT IS	WHY IT HAPPENS	HOW TO OVERCOME IT
Inaction			
Shoulding			
Orthodoxy			
Other Notes			

My Perilous Pitfalls

Now, considering what you just wrote about the basics of the perilous pitfalls, take some time to evaluate how the pitfalls to living and leading purposefully show up for you and then fill out the chart below.

PITFALL	YOUR GO-TO FLAVOR	PREFERRED ANTIDOTE	RECENT EXAMPLE
Inaction	❑ Inertia ❑ Apathy ❑ Fear of failure ❑ Trade-offs ❑ Inconvenient truths ❑ Other:	❑ Start somewhere ❑ Start with my why ❑ Find opportunity ❑ Reward myself ❑ Other:	
Shoulding	❑ Tribal shaming ❑ Conformity ❑ Shoulding myself ❑ Other:	❑ Surround myself with others who model and support purposeful leadership ❑ Share with others my interest in aligning with a larger purpose ❑ Replace traditional *shoulds* with purpose-aligned ones ❑ Be open to failure with a growth mindset ❑ Other:	
Orthodoxy	❑ Conformity bias ❑ Optimal distinctiveness ❑ Shoulding myself ❑ Other:	❑ Shine a light on people who are leading and living purposefully ❑ Strike a balance between inclusion and distinctiveness ❑ Build new norms ❑ Pick my battles ❑ Balance profit and purpose ❑ Other:	

Reflection Questions

Considering how you filled out the chart, which of the pitfalls do you foresee being the biggest challenge for your purpose work and why?

_____

_____

_____

_____

_____

_____

_____

What do you notice about your go-to responses to these pitfalls?

_____

_____

_____

_____

_____

_____

_____

_____

What do you notice about your preferred methods of overcoming these pitfalls?

_____

_____

_____

_____

_____

Looking back at your recent examples, what do you notice now that you didn't realize then about how you deal with obstacles?

_____

_____

_____

_____

_____

What can you start doing right now to prepare yourself for facing each pitfall?

_____

_____

_____

_____

_____

Part 3:

Your Impact
Dashboard

The Self Sphere

It's time! Let's put all your prep work and practice into play and start creating your own Impact Dashboard. We begin with the Self Sphere because it's the most central element of purposeful leadership. This sphere includes all the ways you invest in your physical, intellectual, emotional, and spiritual wellbeing. Without adequate investments here, your purposeful leadership is doomed to fail.

Before you begin your Baseline Assessment for this sphere, take some time to review what you just learned in the book and do some freeform note-taking. Remember, whatever comes to mind is valid.

Chapter 9 Notes

Making It Yours

Now it's time for you to follow the five-step process we talked about in chapter 7 and apply it to your Self Sphere. Below is a reminder of the ABCs of Purposeful Leadership that you'll be applying to each sphere of your Dashboard, followed by the five steps. At the risk of redundancy, I also want to remind you that *perfect is the enemy of good*. Don't overthink your answers.

Awareness

How are you doing in terms of your investments in this sphere? Get a rough estimate.

_____

_____

_____

_____

_____

Belief

Is there a change you can make here that you really believe will increase your wellbeing, performance, and/or fulfillment?

_____

_____

_____

_____

_____

Clarity, Confidence, and Courage

What one activity do you want to add to your activities in this sphere for the next month?

_____

_____

_____

_____

Diving In

What's going to keep you from building that new habit? How can you avoid that pitfall?

_____

_____

_____

_____

Evaluate and Evolve

What's working? What's not? What do you want to celebrate? What do you want to change? Are you seeing and/or feeling your desired impact?

_____

_____

_____

_____

Step 1: Baseline Assessment

Go back to the down and dirty chart or Impact Dashboard Excel Worksheet you made in chapter 7, or wherever you did the work, and review the Self Sphere activities you identified. Edit or add to that list so it feels complete. When you're satisfied that you've captured the activities you do in your Self Sphere, review the total number of hours/percentage of each week you're investing here and add that to the second column. Take one more look at your current activity list. In the fourth column, fill in whether you want to do each activity more, less, or the same.

Now, rate the following statements as they apply to your Self Sphere.

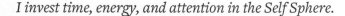

I invest time, energy, and attention in the Self Sphere.

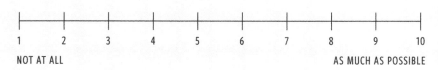

I am satisfied with the quantity and quality of my investments in the Self Sphere.

I see the outcomes of my investments in the Self Sphere.

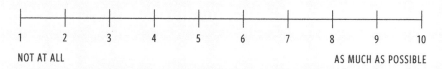

In the table below, record your ratings for today, a year ago, and what you want to aim for a year from now.

	TODAY	1 YEAR AGO	1 YEAR FROM NOW
I invest time, energy, and attention in this sphere.			
I am satisfied with the quantity and quality of investments I make in this sphere.			
I see the outcomes of my investments in this sphere.			

Circle your answers to the questions below.

To hit your one-year target, do you need to do more or less in your Self Sphere?	*More*	*Less*
Do you need to change what you're doing or maintain more of the same?	*Change*	*Maintain*
Do you need to identify new and different Self Sphere activities?	*Yes*	*No*
After seeing the total time you spend on Self Sphere activities, do you want to increase or decrease the hours per week you dedicate to them?	*Increase*	*Decrease*

Summarize your insights.

What are the most powerful investments I'm currently making in my Self Sphere?

_____

_____

_____

What do I want to consider adding to my Self Sphere?

_____

_____

_____

What do I want to consider removing from my Self Sphere?

_____

_____

_____

Step 2: What Do You Need in this Sphere?

What Self Sphere activities are working for you now?

_____

_____

_____

_____

_____

What are you doing that isn't working for you? Why isn't it working? Can you stop or swap it for something else?

In terms of what you're doing and/or who you're doing it with or for, how varied are the investments you make in your Self Sphere?

How would you like to diversify the kinds of activities in this sphere or double down on a few things you already know work or are willing to test out?

What blind spots might you have about the power of investments in the Self Sphere? What people, books, podcasts, or other resources might help reveal these blind spots for you?

_____

_____

_____

_____

_____

Now, draft a belief statement about the investment you want to make in your Self Sphere. Ideally, it will be simple, clear, and measurable. Remember that your belief statement doesn't include exactly _how_ you'll achieve the goal you're setting; you're just identifying _what_ you're going to do and _why_ it matters. If you need some inspiration, review the examples in chapter 9 of the book.

The Clear and Measurable One Thing I'd Like to Try in My Self Sphere:

_____

_____

_____

_____

_____

Step 3: Your Next Step

Based on your work, make a list of the investments you want to make/keep making in your Self Sphere.

ACTIVITIES	HOURS PER WEEK
Total Hours	
Percentage of the week I want to invest in Self Sphere activities	%

Based on your belief about what you want to change, choose your One Thing and get really specific about exactly how to achieve that change. (At least to start; you can always revise the details along the way.)

_____

_____

_____

_____

_____

_____

Now that you know *what* you want to change in your Self Sphere and *why* it matters, let's figure out *how* to achieve that change.

When are you going to do it? For how long?

_____

_____

_____

With whom? (Alone is a fine answer.)

_____

_____

_____

Where are you going to do it?

_____

_____

_____

Do you need any equipment? (If so, do you have it? Do you know where it is? If you don't have it, when and where are you going to acquire it?)

How are you going to hold yourself accountable for doing it (e.g., a habit tracker app, a friend, gold stars on the fridge or your desktop)?

What reward will you give yourself for doing it the first three times and then weekly for keeping it up?

How might you feel after doing this activity regularly for a month?

Step 4: Supporting That Step

Just as having a nonbinding draft of a purpose statement is helpful for focusing on integrating purpose into all you do, having a motivating belief statement helps keep you focused on why you're doing all this purpose work. Your answer to the following questions will help guide you in creating one.

What's going to keep you from building this new habit, whether from the pitfalls or otherwise?

_____

_____

_____

_____

How can you overcome those obstacles?

_____

_____

_____

_____

Write a simple, clear, and measurable behavioral plan to keep you on track. Be sure that this plan connects to the results you want to see from your Self Sphere activities. When you calendar your workout sessions, for example, label them "Sweat for endorphins" or "Stretch for creativity" to remind yourself why you're taking the time to do these activities. For more inspiration, review the examples on page 157 of _Going First_.

My Behavioral Plan for Staying on Track with my Self Sphere Activities:

_____

_____

_____

_____

Now combine your belief statement, behavioral plan, and tracking choice into one succinct paragraph.

The One Thing I'm Going to Start Doing in My Self Sphere and Why:

_____

_____

_____

_____

Step 5: Keep an Eye Out

Next, start preparing a plan and schedule to evolve and evaluate your new habit.

How I'll track it: _____

When and how frequently I'll assess my progress: _____
(add this to your calendar)

What's the impact, or "so what" of this new activity in the Me dimension (your well-being and performance), the We dimension (your family, team, and/or community), and the World dimension (broad scope)?

_____

_____

_____

_____

_____

_____

_____

_____

The Pitfalls of the Self Sphere

Let's review the Self Sphere pitfalls detailed in the book and give you a chance to see how they impact you. What you learn here may add to or modify the insights you've recorded previously. Fill out the pitfall chart below as is relates specifically to your Self Sphere, then journal your answers to the follow-up questions.

PITFALL	YOUR GO-TO FLAVOR	PREFERRED ANTIDOTE	RECENT EXAMPLE
Inaction	☐ Underinvestment (maintain inertia) ☐ Burnout (apathy) ☐ Loss aversion (fear of failure) ☐ Put the needs of others before my own (trade-offs) ☐ Ignore my needs (Inconvenient truths) ☐ Other:	☐ Negotiate (start somewhere) ☐ Reinvest (remember my *why*) ☐ Find opportunities to exercise, rest, etc. ☐ Do what feels good (reward myself) ☐ Find a trade-off ☐ Other:	
Shoulding	☐ Tribal shaming ☐ Maintain the status quo (conformity) ☐ Shoulding myself ☐ Other:	☐ Experiment ☐ Surround myself with others who model a strong balance between self and other activities ☐ Adopt a growth mindset and get comfortable with failure ☐ Rewrite my *shoulds* ☐ Other:	
Orthodoxy	☐ Succumb to having no impact (burnout) ☐ Maintain the status quo (conformity bias) ☐ Underinvest in myself (optimal distinctiveness) ☐ Shoulding myself ☐ Other:	☐ Compile evidence (see it to believe it) ☐ Develop my own tracking practices ☐ Expect more of myself and the people around me ☐ Strike a balance between inclusion and distinctiveness ☐ Focus on my *why* ☐ Build new norms (write a new playbook) ☐ Other:	

How does the pitfall of *inaction* in the Self Sphere impact you the most?

How does inaction in your Self Sphere impact those around you?

In the interest of breaking out of inaction, how will you make your One Thing in the Self Sphere feel good, whether directly in the moment or because of the impact you know it will have?

What are some examples of *shoulding* currently happening in your Self Sphere? Can you think of *shoulds* that you impose on yourself that no one else probably cares about?

What types of tribal shaming do you anticipate when you start this one new Self Sphere habit?

_____

_____

_____

_____

How can you protect this new habit from shoulding?

_____

_____

_____

_____

How can you embrace experimentation in this sphere, adopting a growth mindset and being comfortable with failure? On a scale of 1 (not at all) to 10 (completely). How comfortable are you with experimentation in the Self Sphere? Why did you choose that rating?

_____

_____

_____

_____

What messages do you receive about Self Sphere investments from _orthodoxy_? What orthodox messages do you give yourself?

_____

_____

_____

_____

Crafting Your Self Sphere Cocktail

Crafting your Self Sphere cocktail helps you determine what investments to add and how much of them in order to make your impact the most effective (delicious) it can be. The exact nature and mix of actions in your Self Sphere are truly unique to you, so before crafting yours, consider your answers to these questions:

What are the things that you know help you stay well, whether physically, intellectually, emotionally, or spiritually?

What are things you suspect might help and you'd like to try?

How will you track these activities?

How and how often will you evaluate how they're working for you?

_____

_____

_____

_____

_____

Give your wellness cocktail and/or its component parts a name. For me, meditation is the ice around which the cocktail takes shape; sleep is the mixer; my favorite workout The Class is the spirit; and the workshops, coaching, and other learning is the garnish.

_____

_____

_____

_____

_____

 WANNA SHARE YOUR COCKTAIL OR SEE OTHERS? THAT AND MORE LEARNING IS WHAT THE GOING FIRST COMMUNITY IS FOR!

www.inspiringcowgirl.com/community

Now, on the Spectrum of Impact below, color in your *current* Self Sphere activities; use a different color for your *ideal* ones.

SELF

To stay in touch with how you're feeling in the various dimensions, you have to mix in some review and reflection and then course correct as necessary to make your actions fit your evolving needs. Step back and look at the cocktail you just colored in, considering your Self Sphere holistically one more time. Then answer the following:

What am I doing to invest in my Self Sphere?

_____

_____

_____

_____

_____

What am I not doing that I want to try doing?

_____

_____

_____

_____

_____

_____

What am I doing that I want to stop doing?

_____

_____

_____

_____

_____

Is my "cocktail" blend in this sphere authentic and aligned with my desired impact?

What investments am I making in my Self Sphere that are driven more by shoulding than their actual effects on my well-being?

How do or might the investments in my Self Sphere have impact in the Me, We, and World dimensions?

Overlapping Spheres

Though we learned in the book that there's nothing wrong with investments that sit squarely—and only—in the Self Sphere, in some cases, drawing connections between and among the spheres can be powerful. Pretending that our actions in this area aren't influenced by our context and investments in the other spheres is fruitless because the Self Sphere habits of the people around us influence ours. Take a moment to think about how the activities in your Self Sphere affect your entire Sphere of Impact. It's okay if you don't know for sure yet; just take your best guess.

What connections do your current and desired investments in the Self Sphere have to other spheres?

Family and Friends:

Job:

Workplace:

Community:

Money:

How do you want to revise the investments in your Self Sphere or other spheres to optimize the connections between them?

_____

_____

_____

_____

_____

_____

How can your investments in the Self Sphere multitask by working as investments in other spheres as well? For example, might you commit to better sleep practices with your partner? Make walking meetings a regular team practice? Do a juice cleanse with a friend?

_____

_____

_____

_____

_____

_____

What needs to shift in your other spheres to enable the Self Sphere investments you want to make?

_____

_____

_____

_____

_____

_____

The Family and Friends Sphere

Despite the huge potential influence we can have in the Family and Friends Sphere, our investments there are often overlooked and undervalued by our society, and therefore by ourselves and each other. The people in this sphere are those we choose to love, support, care for, learn from, and grow with. By creating secure attachments, imbuing a growth mindset, fostering a sense of curiosity and empathy, and facilitating a wide variety of experiences for them, we shape (and are shaped by) humans who are more able to lead and live purposefully.

Before you begin your Baseline Assessment for this sphere, take some time to review what you just learned in the book and do some freeform note-taking. Remember, whatever comes to mind is valid.

Chapter 10 Notes

Making It Yours

Now it's time to start crafting your Family and Friends Sphere. If you need a reminder of the ABCs, you can review them in chapter 7.

Step 1: Baseline Assessment

Go back to the down and dirty chart or Impact Dashboard Excel Worksheet you made in chapter 7, or wherever you've been doing the work, and review the Family and Friends activities you identified. Edit or add to that list so it feels complete. When you're satisfied that you've captured the activities you do in your Family and Friends Sphere, review the total number of hours/percentage of each week you're investing here and add that to the second column. Take one more look at your current activity list. In the fourth column, fill in whether you want to do each activity more, less, or the same.

Now, rate the following statements as they apply to your Family and Friends Sphere.

I invest time, energy, and attention in my Family and Friends Sphere.

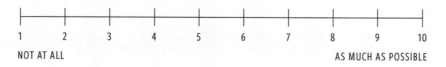

I am satisfied with the quantity and quality of my investments in my Family and Friends Sphere.

I see the outcomes of my investments in my Family and Friends Sphere.

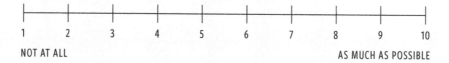

In the table below, record your ratings for today, a year ago, and what you want to aim for a year from now.

	TODAY	1 YEAR AGO	1 YEAR FROM NOW
I invest time, energy, and attention in this sphere.			
I am satisfied with the quantity and quality of investments I make in this sphere.			
I see the outcomes of my investments in this sphere.			

Circle your answers to the questions below.

To hit your one-year target, do you need to do more or less in your Family and Friends Sphere?	*More*	*Less*
Do you need to change what you're doing or maintain more of the same?	*Change*	*Maintain*
Do you need to identify new and different Family and Friends Sphere activities?	*Yes*	*No*
After seeing the total time you spend on Family and Friends Sphere activities, do you want to increase or decrease the hours per week you dedicate to them?	*Increase*	*Decrease*

Summarize your insights.

What are the most powerful investments I'm currently making in my Friends and Family Sphere?

_____

_____

_____

What do I want to consider adding to my Friends and Family Sphere?

_____

_____

_____

What do I want to consider removing from my Friends and Family Sphere?

_____

_____

_____

Step 2: What Do You Need in this Sphere?

What Family and Friends Sphere activities are working for you now?

_____

_____

_____

_____

_____

What are you doing that isn't working for you? Why isn't it working? Can you stop or swap it for something else?

In terms of what you're doing and/or who you're doing it with or for, how varied are the investments you make in your Family and Friends Sphere?

How would you like to diversify the kinds of activities in this sphere or double down on a few things you already know work or are willing to test out?

What blind spots might you have about the power of investments in the Family and Friends Sphere? What people, books, podcasts, or other resources might help reveal these blind spots for you?

_____

_____

_____

_____

_____

Now, draft a simple, clear, and measurable belief statement about the investments you want to make in your Family and Friends Sphere. (Remember, this doesn't include exactly *how*, just *what* and *why*.) If you need some inspiration, review the examples in chapter 10 of the book.

The Clear and Measurable One Thing I'd Like to Try in My Family and Friends Sphere:

_____

_____

_____

_____

_____

Step 3: Your Next Step

Based on your work, make a list of the investments you want to make/keep making in your Family and Friends Sphere.

ACTIVITIES	HOURS PER WEEK
Total Hours	
Percentage of the week I want to invest in Family and Friends Sphere activities	%

Based on your belief about what you want to change, choose *one* thing and get really specific about exactly how to achieve that change. (Again, you can always revise the details along the way.)

_____

_____

_____

_____

_____

Now that you know *what* you want to change in your Family and Friends Sphere and *why* it matters, let's figure out *how* to achieve that change.

When are you going to do it? For how long?

_____

_____

_____

With whom? (Alone is a fine answer.)

_____

_____

_____

Where are you going to do it?

_____

_____

_____

Do you need any equipment? (If so, do you have it? Do you know where it is? If you don't have it, when and where are you going to acquire it?)

_____

_____

_____

How are you going to hold yourself accountable for doing it (e.g., a habit tracker app, a friend, gold stars on the fridge or your desktop)?

_____

_____

_____

What reward will you give yourself for doing it the first three times and then weekly for keeping it up?

_____

_____

_____

How might you feel after doing this activity regularly for a month?

_____

_____

_____

How can you overcome those obstacles?

_____

_____

_____

Write a simple, clear, and measurable behavioral plan to keep you on track. Remember, be sure that this plan connects to the results you want to see from your Family and Friends Sphere activities.

My Behavioral Plan for Staying on Track with My Family and Friends Sphere:

_____

_____

_____

_____

_____

_____

Now combine your belief statement, behavioral plan, and tracking choice into one succinct paragraph.

The One Thing I'm Going to Start Doing in My Family and Friends Sphere and Why:

_____

_____

_____

_____

_____

_____

Step 5: Keep an Eye Out

Next, start preparing a plan and schedule to evolve and evaluate your new habit.

How I'll track it: _____

When and how frequently I'll assess my progress: _____
(add this to your calendar)

What's the impact, or "so what" of this new activity in the Me dimension (your well-being and performance), the We dimension (your family, team, and/or community), and the World dimension (broad scope)?

_____

_____

_____

_____

_____

_____

_____

_____

_____

_____

_____

_____

_____

The Pitfalls of the Family and Friends Sphere

Let's review the Family and Friends Sphere pitfalls detailed in the book and give you a chance to see how they impact you. Remember, what you learn here may add to or modify the insights you've recorded previously. Fill out the pitfall chart below as is relates specifically to your Family and Friends Sphere, and then journal your answers to the follow-up questions.

PITFALL	YOUR GO-TO FLAVOR	PREFERRED ANTIDOTE	RECENT EXAMPLE
Inaction	❑ Miss opportunities (apathy) ❑ Incongruence (trade-offs) ❑ Compartmentalization (inconvenient truths) ❑ Other:	❑ Start somewhere (find opportunities) ❑ Open a conversation ❑ Set my priorities ❑ Remember my *why* ❑ Reward myself ❑ Other:	
Shoulding	❑ Succumb to loneliness ❑ Ignore obligations (succumb to tribal shaming) ❑ Shoulding myself ❑ Other:	❑ Make room for obligations ❑ Make more purposeful connections ❑ Rewrite my *shoulds* ❑ Set new expectations ❑ Other:	
Orthodoxy	❑ Become invisible ❑ Constrain myself and my relationships (conformity; optimal distinctiveness) ❑ Shoulding myself ❑ Other:	❑ Be more intentional ❑ Choose quality over quantity ❑ Track the value of my investments (see it to believe it) ❑ Model and lend my privileges (balance inclusion and distinctiveness) ❑ Other:	

How does the pitfall of *inaction* in the Family and Friends Sphere impact you the most?

How does inaction in your Family and Friends Sphere impact those around you?

In the interest of breaking out of inaction, how will you make your One Thing in the Family and Friends Sphere feel good, whether directly in the moment or because of the impact you know it will have?

What are some examples of *shoulding* currently happening in your Family and Friends Sphere? What will it take to reject some of that shoulding, especially when it isn't aligned with your purpose in this sphere?

What types of tribal shaming do you anticipate when you start this one new Family and Friends Sphere habit?

_____

_____

_____

_____

How can you embrace experimentation in this sphere, adopting a growth mindset and being comfortable with failure? On a scale of 1 (not at all) to 10 (completely), how comfortable are you with experimentation in the Family and Friends Sphere? Why did you choose that rating?

_____

_____

_____

_____

What messages do you receive about Family and Friends Sphere investments from _orthodoxy_? What orthodox messages do you give yourself?

_____

_____

_____

_____

Where are you achieving quantity in your Family and Friends Sphere investments but not quality? What shift would increase the quality of those activities?

_____

_____

_____

_____

What "rules" are you following in your friendships or family that may be outdated and unhelpful? What potential upside(s) might there be to breaking those rules?

How have you allowed your age or life stage to influence the investments you make in your Family and Friends Sphere? How would you like to reverse or change any of those choices, regardless of what your birthdate says you should be doing?

How can you lend your privileges and advantages to your family members or friends? How can they lend theirs to you?

Crafting Your Family and Friends Sphere Cocktail

Crafting your Family and Friends Sphere cocktail helps you determine what investments to add and how much of them in order to make your impact the most effective (delicious) it can be. Like all other sphere cocktails, the exact nature and mix of actions in your Family and Friends Sphere are truly unique to you, so before crafting yours, consider your answers to these questions:

What are the things that you know help you, your family, and your friends stay well, whether physically, intellectually, emotionally, or spiritually?

_____

_____

_____

What are things you suspect might help and you'd like to try?

_____

_____

_____

How will you track these activities?

_____

_____

_____

How and how often will you evaluate how they're working for you?

_____

_____

_____

Give your Family and Friends cocktail and/or its component parts a name.

_____

_____

_____

Now, on the Spectrum of Impact below, color in your *current* Family and Friends Sphere activities; use a different color for your *ideal* ones.

FAMILY   **FRIENDS**

Step back and look at what you just colored in (your cocktail), considering your Family and Friends Sphere holistically one more time. Then answer the following:

What am I doing to invest in my Family and Friends Sphere?

_____

_____

_____

_____

_____

What am I not doing that I want to try doing?

_____

_____

_____

_____

_____

_____

What am I doing that I want to stop doing?

_____

_____

_____

_____

_____

_____

Is my cocktail blend in this sphere authentic and aligned with my desired impact?

_____

_____

_____

_____

_____

What investments am I making in my Family and Friends Sphere that are driven more by shoulding than their actual effects on my wellbeing or the wellbeing of my family and friends?

_____

_____

_____

_____

_____

How do or might the investments in my Family and Friends Sphere affect the Me, We, and World dimensions?

_____

_____

_____

_____

_____

Overlapping Spheres

Take a moment to think about how the activities in your Family and Friends Sphere affect your entire Sphere of Impact. It's okay if you don't know for sure yet; just take your best guess.

What connections do your current and desired investments in the Family and Friends Sphere have to other spheres?

Family and Friends:

Job:

Workplace:

Community:

Money:

How do you want to revise the investments in your Family and Friends Sphere or other spheres to optimize the connections between them?

_____

_____

_____

_____

_____

_____

How can your investments in the Family and Friends Sphere multitask by working as investments in other spheres as well?

_____

_____

_____

_____

_____

_____

What needs to shift in your other spheres to enable the Family and Friends Sphere investments you want to make?

_____

_____

_____

_____

_____

_____

The Job Sphere

The Job Sphere is made up of the professional activities you're somehow compensated for, whether that's money, experience, recognition, room and board, or some other method of reward. Both what you do and how you do it can have rippling positive effects that mirror your values, regardless of where you work. Not feeling good about the impact you're having through your day-to-day work is not a sustainable path forward. There are plenty of ways to have great outcomes and align with your purpose in every single job on the planet, so let's dig in and see how.

Before you begin your Baseline Assessment for this sphere, take some time to review what you just learned in the book and do some freeform note taking. Remember, whatever comes to mind is valid.

Chapter 11 Notes

Making It Yours

It's time to start crafting your Job Sphere. If you need a reminder of the ABCs, you can review them in chapter 7.

Step 1: Baseline Assessment

Go back to the down and dirty chart or Impact Dashboard Excel Worksheet you made in chapter 7, or wherever you've been doing the work, and review the Job Sphere activities you identified. Edit or add to that list so it feels complete. When you're satisfied that you've captured the activities you do in your Job Sphere, review the total number of hours/percentage of each week you're investing here and add that to the second column. Take one more look at your current activity list. In the fourth column, fill in whether you want to do each activity more, less, or the same.

Now, rate the following statements as they apply to your Job Sphere.

I invest time, energy, and attention in my Job Sphere.

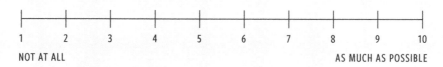

I am satisfied with the quantity and quality of my investments in my Job Sphere.

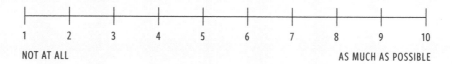

I see the outcomes of my investments in my Job Sphere.

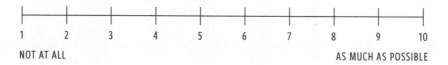

In the table below, record your ratings for today, a year ago, and what you want to aim for a year from now.

	TODAY	1 YEAR AGO	1 YEAR FROM NOW
I invest time, energy, and attention in this sphere.			
I am satisfied with the quantity and quality of investments I make in this sphere.			
I see the outcomes of my investments in this sphere.			

Circle your answer to the questions below.

To hit your one-year target, do you need to do more or less in your Job Sphere?	*More*	*Less*
Do you need to change what you're doing or maintain more of the same?	*Change*	*Maintain*
Do you need to identify new and different Job Sphere activities?	*Yes*	*No*
After seeing the total time you spend on Job Sphere activities, do you want to increase or decrease the hours per week you dedicate to them?	*Increase*	*Decrease*

Summarize your insights.

What are the most powerful investments I'm currently making in my Job Sphere?

_____

_____

_____

What do I want to consider adding to my Job Sphere?

_____

_____

_____

What do I want to consider removing from my Job Sphere?

_____

_____

_____

Step 2: What Do You Need in this Sphere?

What Job Sphere activities are working for you now?

_____

_____

_____

_____

_____

What are you doing that isn't working for you? Why isn't it working? Can you stop or swap it for something else?

In terms of what you're doing and/or who you're doing it with or for, how varied are the investments you make in your Job Sphere?

How would you like to diversify the kinds of activities in this sphere or double down on a few things you already know work or are willing to test out?

What blind spots might you have about the power of investments in the Job Sphere? What people, books, podcasts, or other resources might help reveal these blind spots for you?

_____

_____

_____

_____

_____

_____

_____

Now, draft a simple, clear, and measurable belief statement about the investments you want to make in your Job Sphere. (Remember, this doesn't include exactly _how_, just _what_ and _why_.) If you need some inspiration, review the examples in chapter 11 of the book.

The Clear and Measurable One Thing I'd Like to Try in My Job Sphere:

_____

_____

_____

_____

_____

_____

Step 3: Your Next Step

Based on your work, make a list of the investments you want to make/keep making in your Job Sphere.

ACTIVITIES	HOURS PER WEEK
Total Hours	
Percentage of the week I want to invest in Job Sphere activities	%

Based on your belief about what you want to change, choose *one* thing and get really specific about exactly how to achieve that change. (Again, you can always revise the details along the way.)

_____

_____

_____

_____

_____

_____

Now that you know *what* you want to change in your Job Sphere and *why* it matters, let's figure out *how* to achieve that change.

When are you going to do it? For how long?

_____

_____

_____

With whom? (Alone is a fine answer.)

_____

_____

_____

Where are you going to do it?

_____

_____

_____

Do you need any equipment? (If so, do you have it? Do you know where it is? If you don't have it, when and where are you going to acquire it?)

How are you going to hold yourself accountable for doing it (e.g., a habit tracker app, a friend, gold stars on the fridge or your desktop)?

What reward will you give yourself for doing it the first three times and then weekly for keeping it up?

How might you feel after doing this activity regularly for a month?

Step 4: Supporting That Step

Answer the following questions to help guide you in creating a behavioral plan for staying on track with the activities in your Job Sphere.

What's going to keep you from building this new habit, whether from the pitfalls or otherwise?

_____

_____

_____

How can you overcome those obstacles?

_____

_____

_____

Write a simple, clear, and measurable behavioral plan to keep you on track. Remember, be sure that this plan connects to the results you want to see from your Job Sphere activities.

My Behavioral Plan for Staying on Track with My Job Sphere:

_____

_____

_____

Now combine your belief statement, behavioral plan, and tracking choice into one succinct paragraph.

The One Thing I'm Going to Start Doing in My Job Sphere and Why:

_____

_____

_____

Step 5: Keep an Eye Out

Next, start preparing a plan and schedule to evolve and evaluate your new habit.

How I'll track it: _____

When and how frequently I'll assess my progress: _____
(add this to your calendar)

What's the impact, or "so what" of this new activity in the Me dimension (your well-being and performance), the We dimension (your family, team, and/or community), and the World dimension (broad scope)?

_____

_____

_____

_____

_____

_____

_____

_____

_____

_____

_____

_____

_____

_____

_____

The Pitfalls of the Job Sphere

Let's review the Job Sphere pitfalls detailed in the book and give you a chance to see how they impact you. Remember, what you learn here may add to or modify the insights you've recorded previously. Fill out the pitfall chart below as is relates specifically to your Job Sphere, and then journal your answers to the follow-up questions.

PITFALL	YOUR GO-TO FLAVOR	PREFERRED ANTIDOTE	RECENT EXAMPLE
Inaction	❑ Learned helplessness (inconvenient truths) ❑ Inflexibility (maintain inertia) ❑ The NIMBY effect (apathy) ❑ Other:	❑ Get specific about the outcomes I want to see (start somewhere) ❑ Improve my self-efficacy (remember my *why*) ❑ Be more flexible (look for opportunities) ❑ Better align my job activities with my purpose ❑ Other:	
Shoulding	❑ Default to 20th-century leadership styles (conformity) ❑ React with fear and/or discomfort (tribal shaming) ❑ Shoulding myself ❑ Other:	❑ Follow the Grandmother Rule ❑ Rewrite my *shoulds* ❑ Enlist an accountability buddy ❑ Other:	
Orthodoxy	❑ Lose motivation ❑ Become overwhelmed ❑ Fixate on solutions ❑ Cognitive dissonance ❑ Shoulding myself ❑ Other:	❑ Follow the Grandmother Rule ❑ Do me ❑ Follow my intuition ❑ Talk it up ❑ Adjust my media intake ❑ Other:	

How does the pitfall of *inaction* in the Job Sphere impact you the most?

How does inaction in your Job Sphere impact those around you?

In the interest of breaking out of inaction, how will you make your One Thing in the Job Sphere feel good, whether directly in the moment or because of the impact you know it will have?

What are some examples of *shoulding* currently happening in your Job Sphere? Did you follow along or break with tradition? How did either path feel? Would you do anything differently next time?

What types of tribal shaming do you anticipate when you start this one new Job Sphere habit?

_____

_____

_____

_____

How can you protect this new habit from shoulding?

_____

_____

_____

_____

How can you embrace experimentation in this sphere, adopting a growth mindset and being comfortable with failure? On a scale of 1 (not at all) to 10 (completely), how comfortable are you with experimentation in the Job Sphere? Why did you choose that rating?

_____

_____

_____

_____

What messages do you receive about Job Sphere investments from *orthodoxy*? What orthodox messages do you give yourself?

_____

_____

_____

_____

Identify the skills, talents, experiences, knowledge, and relationships you can bring to your Job Sphere. What assets can you apply to the job tasks you do every day?

How can you adjust your media intake to reduce any overwhelm you might feel by absorbing bad news?

What things are you already doing in your job that you see are making positive change? What low-hanging-fruit activities can you do to contribute more? If you aren't sure how your job tasks connect to your purpose, what colleague can you talk to about it?

Who's your accountability buddy on overcoming shoulding at work? Your grandmother? Dog? Grandchildren? Someone else? How can you trigger yourself to call that person to mind when you're summoning the courage to break away from a *should* to act more purposefully in your Job Sphere?

Crafting Your Job Sphere Cocktail

Crafting your Job Sphere cocktail helps you determine what investments to add and how much of them in order to make your impact the most effective (delicious) it can be. Again, the exact nature and mix of actions in each sphere is truly unique to you, so before crafting yours, consider your answers to these questions:

What are the things that you know help you stay motivated and purposeful with your job duties, whether physically, intellectually, emotionally, or spiritually?

_____

_____

_____

What are things you suspect might help and you'd like to try?

_____

_____

_____

How will you track these activities?

_____

_____

_____

How and how often will you evaluate how they're working for you?

_____

_____

_____

Give your Job Sphere cocktail and/or its component parts a name.

_____

_____

_____

Now, on the Spectrum of Impact below, color in your *current* Job Sphere activities; use a different color for your *ideal* ones.

Step back and look at what you just colored in (your cocktail), considering your Job Sphere holistically one more time. Then answer the following:

What am I doing to invest in my Job Sphere?

_____

_____

_____

_____

_____

What am I not doing that I want to try doing?

_____

_____

_____

_____

_____

What am I doing that I want to stop doing?

_____

_____

_____

_____

_____

_____

Is my cocktail blend in this sphere authentic and aligned with my desired impact?

What investments am I making in my Job Sphere that are driven more by shoulding than their actual effects on my well-being or the well-being of my colleagues?

How do or might the investments in my Job Sphere affect the Me, We, and World dimensions?

Overlapping Spheres

Take a moment to think about how the activities in your Job Sphere affect your entire Sphere of Impact. It's okay if you don't know for sure yet; just take your best guess.

What connections do your current and desired investments in the Job Sphere have to other spheres?

Family and Friends:

Job:

Workplace:

Community:

Money:

How do you want to revise your investments in your Job Sphere or other spheres to optimize the connections between them?

_____

_____

_____

_____

_____

_____

How can your investments in the Job Sphere multitask by working as investments in other spheres as well?

_____

_____

_____

_____

_____

_____

Is there anything that needs to shift in your other spheres to enable the Job Sphere investments you want to make?

_____

_____

_____

_____

_____

_____

CHAPTER 12:

The Workplace Sphere

While the Job Sphere is concerned with what you do and how you perform the duties of your position, the Workplace Sphere represents ways you have impact by virtue of which entity you choose to do that work for and the ways that entity influences the world. The choice of where to work is the primary avenue of impact in the Workplace Sphere because it leads to the secondary avenue of impact: your ability to shape *how* your workplace operates.

Before you begin your Baseline Assessment for this sphere, take some time to review what you just learned in the book and do some freeform note taking. Remember, whatever comes to mind is valid.

Chapter 12 Notes

Making It Yours

It's time to start crafting your Workplace Sphere. If you need a reminder of the ABCs, you can review them in chapter 7.

Step 1: Baseline Assessment

Go back to the down and dirty chart or Impact Dashboard Excel Worksheet you made in chapter 7, or wherever you've been doing the work, and review the Workplace Sphere activities you identified. Edit or add to that list so it feels complete. When you're satisfied that you've captured the activities you do in your Workplace Sphere, review the total number of hours/percentage of each week you're investing here and add that to the second column. Take one more look at your current activity list. In the fourth column, fill in whether you want to do each activity more, less, or the same.

Now, rate the following statements as they apply to your Workplace Sphere.

I invest time, energy, and attention in my Workplace Sphere.

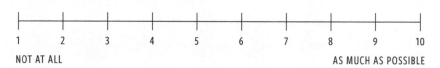

I am satisfied with the quantity and quality of my investments in my Workplace Sphere.

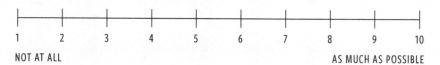

I see the outcomes of my investments in my Workplace Sphere.

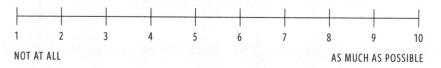

In the table below, record your ratings for today, a year ago, and what you want to aim for a year from now.

	TODAY	1 YEAR AGO	1 YEAR FROM NOW
I invest time, energy, and attention in this sphere.			
I am satisfied with the quantity and quality of investments I make in this sphere.			
I see the outcomes of my investments in this sphere.			

Circle your answer to the questions below.

To hit your one-year target, do you need to do more or less in your Workplace Sphere?	*More*	*Less*
Do you need to change what you're doing or maintain more of the same?	*Change*	*Maintain*
Do you need to identify new and different Workplace Sphere activities?	*Yes*	*No*
After seeing the total time you spend on Workplace Sphere activities, do you want to increase or decrease the hours per week you dedicate to them?	*Increase*	*Decrease*

Summarize your insights.

What are the most powerful investments I'm currently making in my Workplace Sphere?

_____

_____

_____

What do I want to consider adding to my Workplace Sphere?

_____

_____

_____

What do I want to consider removing from my Workplace Sphere?

_____

_____

_____

Step 2: What Do You Need in this Sphere

What Workplace Sphere activities are working for you now?

_____

_____

_____

_____

_____

What are you doing that isn't working for you? Why isn't it working? Can you stop or swap it for something else?

In terms of what you're doing and/or who you're doing it with or for, how varied are the investments you make in your Workplace Sphere?

How would you like to diversify the kinds of activities in this sphere or double down on a few things you already know work or are willing to test out?

What blind spots might you have about the power of investments in the Workplace Sphere? What people, books, podcasts, or other resources might help reveal these blind spots for you?

_____

_____

_____

_____

_____

Now, draft a simple, clear, and measurable belief statement about the investments you want to make in your Workplace Sphere. (Remember, this doesn't include exactly _how_, just _what_ and _why_.) If you need some inspiration, review the examples in chapter 12 of the book.

The Clear and Measurable One Thing I'd Like to Try in My Workplace Sphere:

_____

_____

_____

_____

Step 3: Your Next Step

Based on your work, make a list of the investments you want to make/keep making in your Workplace Sphere.

ACTIVITIES	HOURS PER WEEK
Total Hours	
Percentage of the week I want to invest in Workplace Sphere activities	%

Based on your belief about what you want to change, choose *one* thing and get really specific about exactly how to achieve that change. (Again, you can always revise the details along the way.)

_____

_____

_____

_____

_____

Now that you know *what* you want to change in your Workplace Sphere and *why* it matters, let's figure out *how* to achieve that change.

When are you going to do it? For how long?

_____

_____

_____

With whom? (Alone is a fine answer.)

_____

_____

_____

Where are you going to do it?

_____

_____

_____

Do you need any equipment? (If so, do you have it? Do you know where it is? If you don't have it, when and where are you going to acquire it?)

How are you going to hold yourself accountable for doing it (e.g., a habit tracker app, a friend, gold stars on the fridge or your desktop)?

What reward will you give yourself for doing it the first three times and then weekly for keeping it up?

How might you feel after doing this activity regularly for a month?

Step 4: Supporting That Step

Answer the following questions to help guide you in creating a behavioral plan for staying on track with the activities in your Workplace Sphere.

What's going to keep you from building this new habit, whether from the pitfalls or otherwise?

_____

_____

_____

How can you overcome those obstacles?

_____

_____

_____

Write a simple, clear, and measurable behavioral plan to keep you on track. Remember, be sure that this plan connects to the results you want to see from your Workplace Sphere activities.

My Behavioral Plan for Staying on Track with My Workplace Sphere:

_____

_____

_____

Now combine your belief statement, behavioral plan, and tracking choice into one succinct paragraph.

The One Thing I'm Going to Start Doing in My Workplace Sphere and Why:

_____

_____

_____

Step 5: Keep an Eye Out

Next, start preparing a plan and schedule to evolve and evaluate your new habit.

How I'll track it: _____

When and how frequently I'll assess my progress: _____
(add this to your calendar)

What's the impact, or "so what" of this new activity in the Me dimension (your well-being and performance), the We dimension (your family, team, and/or community), and the World dimension (broad scope)?

_____

_____

_____

_____

_____

_____

_____

_____

_____

_____

_____

_____

_____

_____

The Pitfalls of the Workplace Sphere

Let's review the Workplace Sphere pitfalls detailed in the book and give you a chance to see how they impact you. What you learn here may add to or modify the insights you've recorded previously. Fill out the pitfall chart below as is relates specifically to your Workplace Sphere, and then journal your answers to the follow-up questions.

PITFALL	YOUR GO-TO FLAVOR	PREFERRED ANTIDOTE	RECENT EXAMPLE
Inaction	❑ Succumb to extinction or failure (loss aversion; fear of failure) ❑ Maintain the status quo (inertia) ❑ Other:	❑ Revisit my goals (start somewhere) ❑ Expand my comfort zone (find opportunities) ❑ Enlist my accountability buddy ❑ Use the "yes-and" approach ❑ Become more comfortable with failure in the workplace ❑ Other:	
Shoulding	❑ Misaligned incentives ❑ Mixed messages ❑ Shoulding myself ❑ Other:	❑ Experimentation ❑ Surround myself with purposeful leaders ❑ Adopt a growth mindset ❑ Rewrite my *shoulds* ❑ Other:	
Orthodoxy	❑ Miss opportunities ❑ Cognitive dissonance ❑ Accept the firewalls (conformity) ❑ Shoulding myself ❑ Other:	❑ Evolve my approach ❑ Integrate purpose into my business model ❑ Strike a balance between inclusion and distinctiveness ❑ Contribute to changing the culture in my workplace ❑ Other:	

How does the pitfall of *inaction* in the Workplace Sphere impact you the most?

Do you recognize forms of inaction in your organization? How might that threaten your purpose journey? How is it impacting those around you?

In the interest of breaking out of inaction, how will you make your One Thing in the Workplace Sphere feel good, whether directly in the moment or because of the impact you know it will have?

What are some examples of *shoulding* currently happening in your Workplace Sphere? Which *shoulds* align with your desired impact? Which don't? What's one new *should* that you'd like to bring into your workplace? How will you start?

What types of tribal shaming do you anticipate when you start this one new Workplace Sphere habit?

_____

_____

_____

_____

_____

How can you protect this new habit from shoulding?

_____

_____

_____

_____

_____

How can you embrace experimentation in this sphere, adopting a growth mindset and being comfortable with failure? On a scale of 1 (not at all) to 10 (completely), how comfortable are you with experimentation in the Workplace Sphere? Why did you choose that rating?

_____

_____

_____

_____

_____

What messages do you receive about Workplace Sphere investments from *orthodoxy*? What orthodox messages do you give yourself?

_____

_____

_____

_____

_____

Where might you find a way to update your workplace's *what* or *how* to seize the opportunities of being a yes-and organization, supporting impact as well as business success?

_____

_____

_____

_____

_____

_____

How do you think you should behave as an employee at your workplace?

_____

_____

_____

_____

_____

What script flips can you explore, like Didier's suggestion that we require proof that a non-diverse company performs better? What insights arise from that thought experiment?

_____

_____

_____

_____

_____

How do you feel about the work you do when you talk about it with others? When has it been uncomfortable because of a values misalignment or particularly fulfilling to bring up your workplace in a personal setting?

_____

_____

_____

_____

_____

What's one first step you can take toward investigating or activating opportunities for integration of profit and purpose in your workplace?

_____

_____

_____

_____

_____

Crafting Your Workplace Sphere Cocktail

Crafting your Workplace Sphere cocktail helps you determine what investments to add and how much of them in order to make your impact the most effective (delicious) it can be. Before crafting yours, consider your answers to these questions:

What are the things that you know help your workplace culture stay well, whether physically, intellectually, emotionally, or spiritually?

What are things you suspect might help and you'd like to try?

How will you track these activities?

How and how often will you evaluate how they're working for you?

Give your Job Sphere cocktail and/or its component parts a name.

_____

_____

_____

Now, on the Spectrum of Impact below, color in your *current* Workplace Sphere activities; use a different color for your *ideal* ones.

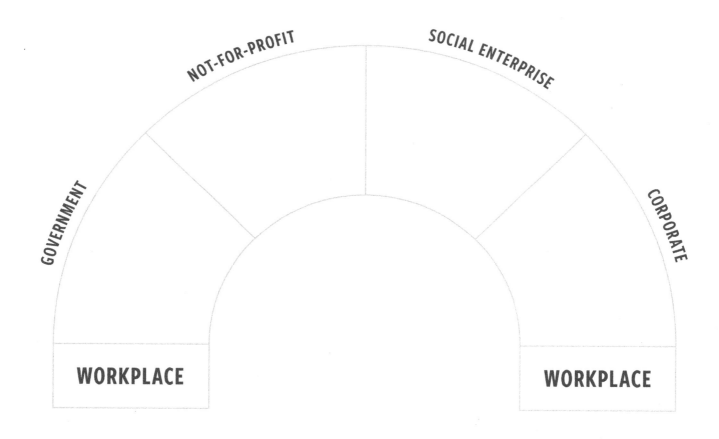

Step back and look at what you just colored in (your cocktail), considering your Workplace Sphere holistically one more time. Then answer the following:

What am I doing to invest in my Workplace Sphere?

_____

_____

_____

_____

_____

What am I not doing that I want to try doing?

_____

_____

_____

_____

_____

_____

What am I doing that I want to stop doing?

_____

_____

_____

_____

_____

Is my cocktail blend in this sphere authentic and aligned with my desired impact?

_____

_____

_____

_____

_____

What investments am I making in my Workplace Sphere that are driven more by shoulding than their actual effects on my well-being or the well-being of others in my workplace?

_____

_____

_____

_____

_____

How do or might the investments in my Workplace Sphere affect the Me, We, and World dimensions?

_____

_____

_____

_____

_____

Overlapping Spheres

Take a moment to think about how the activities in your Workplace Sphere affect your entire Sphere of Impact. It's okay if you don't know for sure yet; just take your best guess.

What connections do your current and desired investments in the Workplace Sphere have to other spheres?

Family and Friends:

Job:

Workplace:

Community:

Money:

How do you want to revise the investments in your Workplace Sphere or other spheres to optimize the connections between them?

_____

_____

_____

_____

_____

How can your investments in the Workplace Sphere multitask by working as investments in other spheres as well?

_____

_____

_____

_____

_____

_____

What needs to shift in your other spheres to enable the Workplace Sphere investments you want to make?

_____

_____

_____

_____

_____

CHAPTER 13:

The Community Sphere

Community activities can be a healthy and productive complement to our lives and work, particularly if our current job or workplace doesn't provide the level of impact we're seeking. These "extracurricular activities" are also a great chance to expand our networks, build new skills, learn new industries, and have more of the positive influence that creates a meaningful life. Having a sense of community can also be a particularly important comfort during times of uncertainty.

Community is often the most sparsely populated sphere, even among purposeful leaders, so let's explore what this sphere looks like for you. Before you begin your Baseline Assessment, take some time to review what you just learned in the book and do some freeform note taking. Remember, whatever comes to mind is valid.

Chapter 13 Notes

Making It Yours

It's time to start crafting your Community Sphere. If you need a reminder of the ABCs, you can review them in chapter 7.

Step 1: Baseline Assessment

Go back to the down and dirty chart or Impact Dashboard Excel Worksheet you made in chapter 7, or wherever you've been doing the work, and review the Community Sphere activities you identified. Edit or add to that list so it feels complete. When you're satisfied that you've captured the activities you do in your Community Sphere, review the total number of hours/percentage of each week you're investing here and add that to the second column. Take one more look at your current activity list. In the fourth column, fill in whether you want to do each activity more, less, or the same.

Now, rate the following statements as they apply to your Community Sphere.

I invest time, energy, and attention in my Community Sphere.

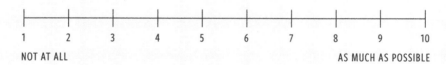

I am satisfied with the quantity and quality of my investments in my Community Sphere.

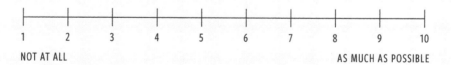

I see the outcomes of my investments in my Community Sphere.

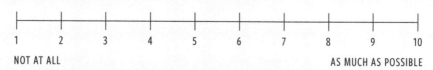

In the table below, record your ratings for today, a year ago, and what you want to aim for a year from now.

	TODAY	1 YEAR AGO	1 YEAR FROM NOW
I invest time, energy, and attention in this sphere.			
I am satisfied with the quantity and quality of investments I make in this sphere.			
I see the outcomes of my investments in this sphere.			

Circle your answer to the questions below.

To hit your one-year target, do you need to do more or less in your Community Sphere?	*More*	*Less*
Do you need to change what you're doing or maintain more of the same?	*Change*	*Maintain*
Do you need to identify new and different Community Sphere activities?	*Yes*	*No*
After seeing the total time you spend on Community Sphere activities, do you want to increase or decrease the hours per week you dedicate to them?	*Increase*	*Decrease*

Summarize your insights.

What are the most powerful investments I'm currently making in my Community Sphere?

_____

_____

_____

What do I want to consider adding to my Community Sphere?

_____

_____

_____

What do I want to consider removing from my Community Sphere?

_____

_____

_____

Step 2: What Do You Need in this Sphere?

What Community Sphere activities are working for you now?

_____

_____

_____

_____

_____

What are you doing that isn't working for you? Why isn't it working? Can you stop or swap it for something else?

In terms of what you're doing and/or who you're doing it with or for, how varied are the investments you make in your Community Sphere?

How would you like to diversify the kinds of activities in this sphere or double down on a few things you already know work or are willing to test out?

What blind spots might you have about the power of investments in the Community Sphere? What people, books, podcasts, or other resources might help reveal these blind spots for you?

_____

_____

_____

_____

_____

Now, draft a simple, clear, and measurable belief statement about the investments you want to make in your Community Sphere. (Remember, this doesn't include exactly _how_, just _what_ and _why_.) If you need some inspiration, review the examples in chapter 13 of the book.

The Clear and Measurable One Thing I'd Like to Try in My Community Sphere:

_____

_____

_____

_____

_____

Step 3: Your Next Step

Based on your work, make a list of the investments you want to make/keep making in your Community Sphere.

ACTIVITIES	HOURS PER WEEK
Total Hours	
Percentage of the week I want to invest in Community Sphere activities	%

Based on your belief about what you want to change, choose *one* thing and get really specific about exactly how to achieve that change. (Again, you can always revise the details along the way.)

_____

_____

_____

_____

_____

Now that you know *what* you want to change in your Community Sphere and *why* it matters, let's figure out *how* to achieve that change.

When are you going to do it? For how long?

_____

_____

_____

With whom? (Alone is a fine answer.)

_____

_____

_____

Where are you going to do it?

_____

_____

_____

Do you need any equipment? (If so, do you have it? Do you know where it is? If you don't have it, when and where are you going to acquire it?)

How are you going to hold yourself accountable for doing it (e.g., a habit tracker app, a friend, gold stars on the fridge or your desktop)?

What reward will you give yourself for doing it the first three times and then weekly for keeping it up?

How might you feel after doing this activity regularly for a month?

Step 4: Supporting That Step

Answer the following questions to help guide you in creating a behavioral plan for staying on track with the activities in your Community Sphere.

What's going to keep you from building this new habit, whether from the pitfalls or otherwise?

_____

_____

_____

How can you overcome those obstacles?

_____

_____

Write a simple, clear, and measurable behavioral plan to keep you on track. Remember, be sure that this plan connects to the results you want to see from your Community Sphere activities.

My Behavioral Plan for Staying on Track with My Community Sphere:

_____

_____

Now combine your belief statement, behavioral plan, and tracking choice into one succinct paragraph.

The One Thing I'm Going to Start Doing in My Community Sphere and Why:

_____

_____

_____

Step 5: Keep an Eye Out

Next, start preparing a plan and schedule to evolve and evaluate your new habit.

How I'll track it: _____

When and how frequently I'll assess my progress: _____
(add this to your calendar)

What's the impact, or "so what" of this new activity in the Me dimension (your well-being and performance), the We dimension (your family, team, and/or community), and the World dimension (broad scope)?

_____

_____

_____

_____

_____

_____

_____

_____

_____

_____

_____

_____

_____

_____

The Pitfalls of the Community Sphere

Let's review the Community Sphere pitfalls detailed in the book and give you a chance to see how they impact you. What you learn here may add to or modify the insights you've recorded previously. Fill out the pitfall chart below as is relates specifically to your Community Sphere, and then journal your answers to the follow-up questions.

PITFALL	YOUR GO-TO FLAVOR	PREFERRED ANTIDOTE	RECENT EXAMPLE
Inaction	❑ Fragility ❑ Isolation ❑ Miss opportunities ❑ Stick to what I know (fear of failure) ❑ Other:	❑ Consider my social capital (start somewhere) ❑ Increase and/or expand my engagement (find opportunities) ❑ Leverage my unique skill(s) or knowledge ❑ Other:	
Shoulding	❑ Staying in my comfort zone ❑ Tribal shaming ❑ Shoulding myself ❑ Other:	❑ Reach beyond my comfort zone ❑ Start building my community/social capital ❑ Surround myself with purposeful leaders in my community ❑ Try something new ❑ Rewrite my *shoulds* ❑ Other:	
Orthodoxy	❑ Homogeneity (conformity) ❑ Follow the status quo (optimal distinctiveness) ❑ Shoulding myself ❑ Other:	❑ Build bridges ❑ Find a good match ❑ Thoughtful problem-solving ❑ Look for win-win-wins ❑ Look beyond not-for-profits ❑ Other:	

How does the pitfall of *inaction* in the Community Sphere impact you the most?

How does inaction in your Community Sphere impact those around you?

In the interest of breaking out of inaction, how will you make your One Thing in the Community Sphere feel good, whether directly in the moment or because of the impact you know it will have?

What are some examples of *shoulding* currently happening in your Community Sphere?

What types of tribal shaming do you anticipate when you start this one new Community Sphere habit?

_____

_____

_____

_____

_____

How can you protect this new habit from shoulding?

_____

_____

_____

_____

_____

How can you embrace experimentation in this sphere, adopting a growth mindset and being comfortable with failure? On a scale of 1 (not at all) to 10 (completely), how comfortable are you with experimentation in the Community Sphere? Why did you choose that rating?

_____

_____

_____

_____

_____

What messages do you receive about Community Sphere investments from *orthodoxy*? What orthodox messages do you give yourself?

Where are you currently in terms of isolation versus engagement with your community, whether that's local, global, or simply being united by common interests? What impact on yourself or your community might result if you engaged more (or less, if you're feeling overcommitted)?

As you review your Community Sphere investments, which ones have you "grown out of" or aren't providing the same joy they used to? On the opposite extreme, is there something lurking beneath the surface that you think you might like to do but haven't?

What's one area in which you'd like to diversify your community? Are there ways you can contribute to or learn from that community group? What do you want to contribute? Your time? Your money? Your social connections?

_____

_____

_____

_____

_____

_____

_____

What are you hoping to gain from your community investments? Are you clear on those expectations and ready to have an honest conversation with your potential community partners about them?

_____

_____

_____

_____

_____

_____

Have you explored ways beyond not-for-profits to have the impact you seek? If not, where might you learn about these alternate paths to change?

_____

_____

_____

_____

_____

Crafting Your Community Sphere Cocktail

Crafting your Community Sphere cocktail helps you determine what investments to add and how much of them in order to make your impact the most effective (delicious) it can be. The exact nature and mix of actions are truly unique to you, so before crafting yours, consider your answers to these questions:

What are the things that you know help your community stay well, whether physically, intellectually, emotionally, or spiritually?

What are things you suspect might help and you'd like to try?

How will you track these activities?

How and how often will you evaluate how they're working for you?

Give your Community Sphere cocktail and/or its component parts a name.

_____

_____

_____

Now, on the Spectrum of Impact below, color in your *current* Community Sphere activities; use a different color for your *ideal* ones.

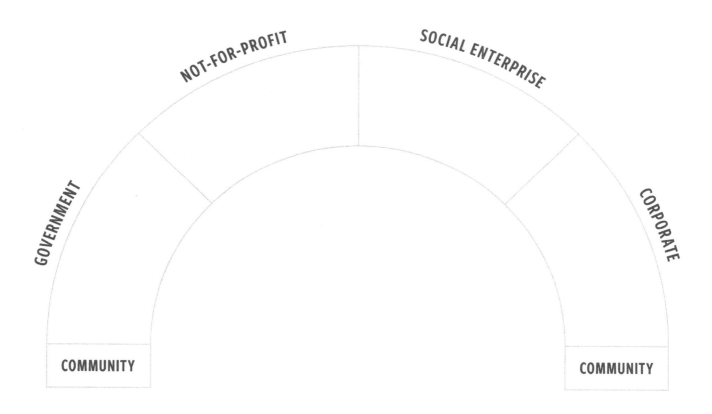

Step back and look at what you just colored in (your cocktail), considering your Community Sphere holistically one more time. Then answer the following:

What am I doing to invest in my Community Sphere?

_____

_____

_____

_____

_____

What am I not doing that I want to try doing?

_____

_____

_____

_____

_____

What am I doing that I want to stop doing?

_____

_____

_____

_____

_____

Is my cocktail blend in this sphere authentic and aligned with my desired impact?

_____

_____

_____

_____

_____

What investments am I making in my Community Sphere that are driven more by shoulding than their actual effects on my well-being or the well-being of those in my community?

_____

_____

_____

_____

_____

How do or might the investments in my Community Sphere affect the Me, We, and World dimensions?

_____

_____

_____

_____

_____

Overlapping Spheres

Take a moment to think about how the activities in your Community Sphere affect your entire Sphere of Impact. It's okay if you don't know for sure yet; just take your best guess.

What connections do your current and desired investments in the Workplace Sphere have to other spheres?

Family and Friends:

Job:

Workplace:

Community:

Money:

How do you want to revise the investments in your Community or other spheres to optimize the connections between them?

_____

_____

_____

_____

_____

How can your investments in the Community Sphere multitask by working as investments in other spheres as well?

_____

_____

_____

_____

_____

Is there anything that needs to shift in your other spheres to enable the Community Sphere investments you want to make?

_____

_____

_____

_____

_____

The Money, Money, Money Sphere

When it comes to your Impact Dashboard, money means far more than simply affording the costs of fixing the problems you care about. Money is merely a way of facilitating exchange. It enables certain activities to continue (or not) and needs to be the servant of our desired outcomes, not the master. To truly have the impact you seek, you need to make purposeful choices about how you allocate your money. As with all of your investments of time, energy, and attention, the important thing is to align your expectations of returns.

Before you begin your Baseline Assessment for this sphere, take some time to review what you just learned in the book and do some freeform note taking. Remember, whatever comes to mind is valid.

Chapter 14 Notes

Making It Yours

It's time to start crafting your Money Sphere. If you need a reminder of the ABCs, you can review them in chapter 7.

Step 1: Baseline Assessment

Go back to the down and dirty chart or Impact Dashboard Excel Worksheet you made in chapter 7, or wherever you've been doing the work, and review the Money Sphere activities you identified. Edit or add to that list so it feels complete. When you're satisfied that you've captured the activities you do in your Money Sphere, review the total number of hours/percentage of each week you're investing here and add that to the second column. Take one more look at your current activity list. In the fourth column, fill in whether you want to do each activity more, less, or the same.

Now, rate the following statements as they apply to your Money Sphere.

I invest time, energy, and attention in my Money Sphere.

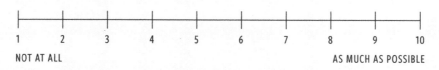

I am satisfied with the quantity and quality of my investments in my Money Sphere.

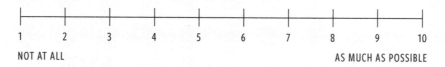

I see the outcomes of my investments in my Money Sphere.

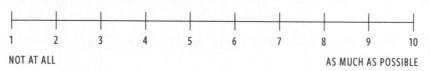

In the table below, record your ratings for today, a year ago, and what you want to aim for a year from now.

	TODAY	1 YEAR AGO	1 YEAR FROM NOW
I invest time, energy, and attention in this sphere.			
I am satisfied with the quantity and quality of investments I make in this sphere.			
I see the outcomes of my investments in this sphere.			

Circle your answer to the questions below.

To hit your one-year target, do you need to do more or less in your Money Sphere?	*More*	*Less*
Do you need to change what you're doing or maintain more of the same?	*Change*	*Maintain*
Do you need to identify new and different Money Sphere activities?	*Yes*	*No*
After seeing the total time you spend on Money Sphere activities, do you want to increase or decrease the hours per week you dedicate to them?	*Increase*	*Decrease*

Summarize your insights.

What are the most powerful investments I'm currently making in my Money Sphere?

_____

_____

_____

What do I want to consider adding to my Money Sphere?

_____

_____

_____

What do I want to consider removing from my Money Sphere?

_____

_____

_____

Step 2: What Do You Need in this Sphere?

What Money Sphere activities are working for you now?

_____

_____

_____

_____

_____

What are you doing that isn't working for you? Why isn't it working? Can you stop or swap it for something else?

In terms of what you're doing and/or who you're doing it with or for, how varied are the investments you make in your Money Sphere?

How would you like to diversify the kinds of activities in this sphere or double down on a few things you already know work or are willing to test out?

What blind spots might you have about the power of investments in the Money Sphere? What people, books, podcasts, or other resources might help reveal these blind spots for you?

_____

_____

_____

_____

_____

Now, draft a simple, clear, and measurable belief statement about the investments you want to make in your Money Sphere. (Remember, this doesn't include exactly _how_, just _what_ and _why_.) If you need some inspiration, review the examples in chapter 14 of the book.

The Clear and Measurable One Thing I'd Like to Try in My Money Sphere:

_____

_____

_____

_____

_____

_____

Step 3: Your Next Step

Based on your work, make a list of the investments you want to make/keep making in your Money Sphere.

ACTIVITIES	HOURS PER WEEK
Total Hours	
Percentage of the week I want to invest in Money Sphere activities	%

Based on your belief about what you want to change, choose *one* thing and get really specific about exactly how to achieve that change. (Again, you can always revise the details along the way.)

_____

_____

_____

_____

_____

_____

Now that you know *what* you want to change in your Money Sphere and *why* it matters, let's figure out *how* to achieve that change.

When are you going to do it? For how long?

_____

_____

_____

With whom? (Alone is a fine answer.)

_____

_____

_____

Where are you going to do it?

_____

_____

_____

Do you need any equipment? (If so, do you have it? Do you know where it is? If you don't have it, when and where are you going to acquire it?)

_____

_____

_____

_____

How are you going to hold yourself accountable for doing it (e.g., a habit tracker app, a friend, gold stars on the fridge or your desktop)?

_____

_____

_____

_____

What reward will you give yourself for doing it the first three times and then weekly for keeping it up?

_____

_____

_____

_____

How might you feel after doing this activity regularly for a month?

_____

_____

_____

_____

Step 4: Supporting That Step

Answer the following questions to help guide you in creating a behavioral plan for staying on track with the activities in your Money Sphere.

What's going to keep you from building this new habit, whether from the pitfalls or otherwise?

_____

_____

_____

How can you overcome those obstacles?

_____

_____

_____

Write a simple, clear, and measurable behavioral plan to keep you on track. Remember, be sure that this plan connects to the results you want to see from your Money Sphere activities.

My Behavioral Plan for Staying on Track with My Money Sphere:

_____

_____

_____

Now combine your belief statement, behavioral plan, and tracking choice into one succinct paragraph.

The One Thing I'm Going to Start Doing in My Money Sphere and Why:

_____

_____

_____

Step 5: Keep an Eye Out

Next, start preparing a plan and schedule to evolve and evaluate your new habit.

How I'll track it: _____

When and how frequently I'll assess my progress: _____
(add this to your calendar)

What's the impact, or "so what" of this new activity in the Me dimension (your well-being and performance), the We dimension (your family, team, and/or community), and the World dimension (broad scope)?

_____

_____

_____

_____

_____

_____

_____

_____

_____

_____

_____

_____

_____

The Pitfalls of the Money Sphere

Let's review the Money Sphere pitfalls detailed in the book and give you a chance to see how they impact you. What you learn here may add to or modify the insights you've recorded previously. Fill out the pitfall chart below as is relates specifically to your Money Sphere, and then journal your answers to the follow-up questions.

PITFALL	YOUR GO-TO FLAVOR	PREFERRED ANTIDOTE	RECENT EXAMPLE
Inaction	❏ Market failure ❏ Surrender my financial power ❏ Give up some things for others (trade-offs) ❏ Other:	❏ Harness my buying power (start somewhere) ❏ Reallocate my donations and investments to align them with my values (focus on my why) ❏ Use the KonMari Method™ ❏ Speak up as an investor ❏ Other:	
Shoulding	❏ Make poor decisions ❏ Focus only monetary elements of success ❏ Immediacy bias ❏ Primary bias ❏ Dissatisfaction ❏ Shoulding myself ❏ Other:	❏ Expand my focus to more than financial benefits ❏ Better account for both risk and reward ❏ Holistic decision-making ❏ Consider my activity along the entire Spectrum of Impact ❏ Rewrite my *shoulds* ❏ Other:	
Orthodoxy	❏ Restrict myself and my activities ❏ Keep blinders on ❏ Shoulding myself ❏ Other:	❏ Look for opportunities to do good *and* do well ❏ Build accountability into my business model ❏ Remove my blinders (see it to believe it) ❏ Better integrate my Spectrum of capital with my purpose ❏ Develop a holistic view about money (challenge the norms) ❏ Other:	

How does the pitfall of *inaction* in the Money Sphere impact you the most?

How does inaction in your Money Sphere impact those around you?

In the interest of breaking out of inaction, how will you make your One Thing in the Money Sphere feel good, whether directly in the moment or because of the impact you know it will have?

What are some examples of *shoulding* currently happening in your Money Sphere? Which *shoulds* would you like to let go of in this sphere?

What type of tribal shaming do you anticipate when you start this one new Money Sphere habit? If so, in what way?

How can you protect this new habit from shoulding?

How can you embrace experimentation in this sphere, adopting a growth mindset and being comfortable with failure? On a scale of 1 (not at all) to 10 (completely), how comfortable are you with experimentation in the Money Sphere? Why did you choose that rating?

What messages do you receive about Money Sphere investments from *orthodoxy*? What orthodox messages do you give yourself?

_____

_____

_____

_____

How might you be giving up your financial power as a consumer, investor, or donor? What are you doing to drive results by what you buy, invest in, and donate to? What are you not doing?

_____

_____

_____

_____

What choices do you already make about how to use your money in order to better align your values with your desired outcomes?

_____

_____

_____

_____

Do you feel like your money is working for you? More specifically, do you feel like it's working for your desired results? Why or why not?

_____

_____

_____

_____

How distributed or concentrated is your money across your Spectrum of Capital? What's one use of money you can make today at a point on the Spectrum where you're currently underinvested?

_____

_____

_____

_____

_____

What nonfinancial outcomes do you want from your income or savings? What Money Sphere activities can you invest in that would lead to those outcomes? For example, is it important to you to learn a new language or visit your parents annually? Do you want to fund mental health care for a certain group of people or donate annually to candidates with an identity or platform you support?

_____

_____

_____

_____

_____

When was the last time you audited your grocery shopping process? Review your weekly purchases and ask yourself what you can buy from local shops or brands, which items you can replace with a B Corp or other certified "for-good" business, and what choices you can make that reduce the disposable packaging you buy. Think about groceries, clothing, gifts, and entertainment.

_____

_____

_____

_____

_____

Crafting Your Money Sphere Cocktail

Crafting your Money Sphere cocktail helps you determine what investments to add and how much of them in order to make your impact the most effective (delicious) it can be. The exact nature and mix of actions is truly unique to you, so before crafting yours, consider your answers to these questions:

What are the things that you know help you stay well financially?

How will you track these activities?

What are things you suspect might help and you'd like to try?

How will you track these activities?

How and how often will you evaluate how they're working for you?

Give your Money Sphere cocktail and/or its component parts a name.

_____

_____

_____

Now, on the Spectrum of Impact below, color in your *current* Money Sphere activities; use a different color for your *ideal* ones.

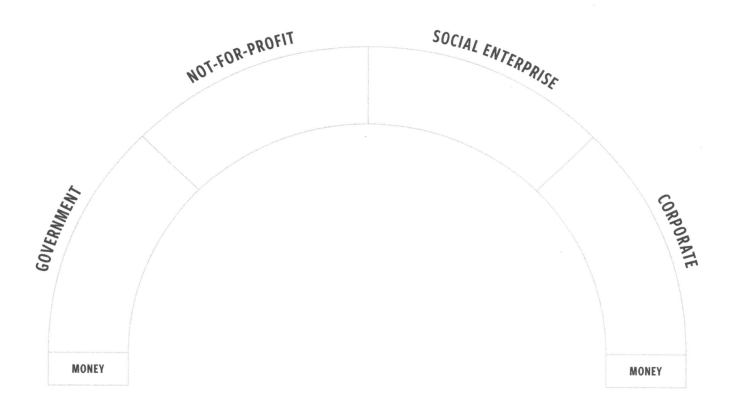

Step back and look at what you just colored in (your cocktail), considering your Money Sphere holistically one more time. Then answer the following:

What am I doing to invest in my Money Sphere?

_____

_____

_____

_____

_____

_____

What am I not doing that I want to try doing?

_____

_____

_____

_____

_____

_____

What am I doing that I want to stop doing?

_____

_____

_____

_____

_____

_____

Is my cocktail blend in this sphere authentic and aligned with my desired impact?

_____

_____

_____

_____

_____

Where am I making investments in my Money Sphere that are driven more by shoulding than their actual effects on my well-being?

_____

_____

_____

_____

_____

How do or might the investments in my Money Sphere affect the Me, We, and World dimensions?

_____

_____

_____

_____

_____

Overlapping Spheres

Take a moment to think about how the activities in your Money Sphere affect your entire Sphere of Impact. It's okay if you don't know for sure yet; just take your best guess.

What connections do your current and desired investments in the Money Sphere have to other spheres?

Family and Friends:

Job:

Workplace:

Community:

Money:

How do you want to revise the investments in your Money Sphere, or other spheres, to optimize the connections between them?

_____

_____

_____

_____

_____

How can your investments in the Money Sphere multitask by working as investments in other spheres as well?

_____

_____

_____

_____

_____

What needs to shift in your other spheres to enable the Money Sphere investments you want to make?

_____

_____

_____

_____

_____

The Party Is Just Beginning

It's finally time to put it all together and throw a Purpose Party! By now you've learned that the party requires your active participation; it's not a one-directional, switch-it-on-and-off performance but an interactive, day in/day out approach to your work and life. By actively participating in the Purpose Party, you create a ripple effect that extends from Me to We to World. With your participation, we can properly align two major problems—the urgent need for sustainable, strategic solutions to social and environmental problems and people's need to have positive impact in their work—to solve each other. The outcome will be a win-win-win: individuals will be happier, healthier, more motivated and fulfilled; their teams and organizations will be more productive, innovative, and efficient thanks to a more engaged, inspired, creative, and collaborative workforce; and people and the planet will benefit from the positive results created.

Chapter 15 Notes

Where We Began

Evolving and evaluating is a critical step when making your Dashboard come to life. Take a minute to review your answers to the reflection questions presented in the introduction and chapters 1 and 2 of this playbook.

Are you still afraid of Going First? Why or why not?

_____

_____

_____

Has your definition of or feelings about purpose changed? If so, how?

_____

_____

_____

Has your purpose statement changed? If so, how?

_____

_____

_____

Did I answer that #1 question of yours? (If not, feel free to submit it to me on my website and I'll do my best!)

_____

_____

_____

Looking back at the *one* thing in your life that you hoped to change by reading *Going First* and working with this playbook, how close are you to changing it?

_____

_____

_____

How has your commitment to working with this material each week been going?

_____

_____

_____

How has this purpose work affected your readiness to accept the mission?

_____

_____

_____

It might also be helpful to revisit this quick video with my guidance on maximizing your Purpose Party Playbook experience, as you near the end [of this first round!] of your work through it. It'll remind you what you might have missed this time around, or where you want to go next in your growth as a purposeful leader.

 MAXIMIZE YOUR PURPOSE PARTY PLAYBOOK EXPERIENCE

www.inspiringcowgirl.com/playbook

Living Your Dashboard for Win-Win-Wins

Now that you've reflected on your purpose journey, it's time to put it all together and create your living Impact Dashboard. We'll start by considering the ripple effect you're creating by living and leading purposefully, which will help keep you motivated. The consequences of your efforts—your "so what"—fall into the three dimensions of Me, We, and World.

Take a look at look at the six One Things you're aiming to start doing to have more of the impact you seek and consider the outcomes of those purposeful activities. In the chart below, fill in how your six One Things are, have been, and/or will be impacting each dimension. For example, if one of your goals is to shape *how* your workplace operates, consider the organization's mission and how it creates impact in each of the three dimensions.

Me:

My workplace is supporting my well-being and performance by...

_____

_____

We:

My workplace is supporting my desired impact on my team, my family and friends, and my community by...

_____

_____

World:

My workplace is supporting my desired impact on the world by...It's okay if you don't know yet what the outcomes of your purposeful sphere investments are or will be. The very process of envisioning these outcomes is what creates an upward spiral of win-win-wins.

_____

_____

MY "ONE THING"	WIN #1: ME	WIN #2: WE	WIN #3: WORLD
Self Sphere			
Family and Friends Sphere			
Job Sphere			
Workplace Sphere			
Community Sphere			
Money Sphere			

Prioritizing Your Next Steps

Now that you've identified your "so what" of the six main investments you want to make in each Sphere of Impact, you need to prioritize them. Start by jotting down a few things that are working for you with each investment and a few ideas you can consider implementing.

_____

_____

_____

_____

_____

_____

_____

_____

_____

Now, let's prioritize. I recommend starting with the One Thing you're most excited about starting because it will help build momentum and keep you motivated:

1. _____

2. _____

3. _____

4. _____

5. _____

6. _____

Now, draw them on this blank dashboard, with numbers for priority.

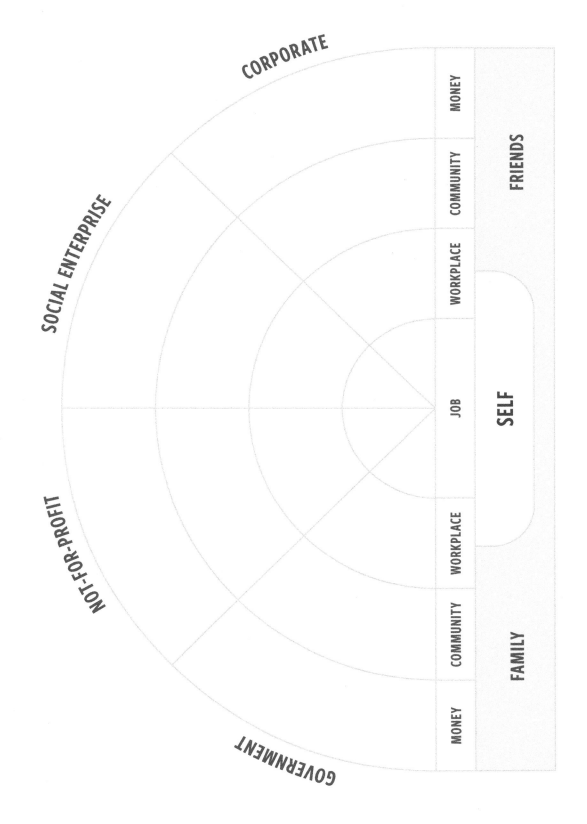

Next, open the Impact Dashboard Excel Worksheet, and go to the Purpose Party Planner tab. If you're not using my Excel template, go back through wherever you've been working through the dashboard, and compile the six One Things from each Sphere, and prioritize them. Which will you work on first, based on its urgency, fit with other things happening in the next two months, and so on. This will set your efforts over the next six quarters, which will come in handy while you track your progress and evolve what you're doing over time.

Your Notes

Purpose Party Host Tips

So now you've got your priorities set and know your why for throwing a Purpose Party. Great! Almost there. The next step is to turn your priorities into habits so you can keep your Dashboard alive. To prepare, consider how these three tips are most relevant to you in building your new habits, given what you know about your fears, pitfalls, and motivations.

Avoid perfection

Establish boundaries

Invite your people

Making the Party Last: Building Strong Habits

Your Impact Dashboard is a lifelong guide, intended to be drafted, revisited, revised, and even restarted many times throughout your life. It can and should shift over time, increasing the emphasis on some spheres over others or some activities within a certain sphere. Your Dashboard will typically shift along with the habits you build. To reinforce those habits, it's essential to keep checking in with yourself.

Remember, too, that when tracking your purpose journey, it's important to capture not only quantitative data (how often did I do the thing) but also qualitative information (how did it make me feel and what effect did it have) about your new purposeful habit(s).

How will you record this qualitative information? A journal? Quarterly updates with yourself? Quiet reflection sessions?

_____

_____

_____

_____

_____

What will you need on hand to do this, and how might you stay motivated?

_____

_____

_____

_____

_____

With that in mind, here are some daily, weekly, monthly, and yearly processes for tracking your success.

Daily Review

It's crucial to find some way to interact with your Dashboard on a daily basis so it becomes integrated into your everyday choices and behaviors. This daily practice can be as simple as putting a sticky note on your mirror or adding a background image on your phone or laptop that reminds you of the sphere of focus for the quarter. It could be asking yourself what you'll do today in that sphere while you brush your teeth or taking a quick inventory of all six spheres as you look at your calendar for the day.

Just as perfect is the enemy of good, complex is the enemy of regularity. Choose a simple daily action and try it out. Many people enjoy using a habit tracker or journaling app (see my favorites at www.inspiringcowgirl.com/tools) to record their progress on any daily practice.

The daily check-in I think will work for me best is:

The way I will trigger myself to do it is:

Weekly/Monthly Review

It's helpful to have a regularly scheduled check-in with your Dashboard too. You could even pair it with something that you're already doing. For example, do you have a weekly team meeting that you can tack 10 minutes onto to review your Dashboard? A monthly bill-paying session you can reward yourself for by spending 20–30 minutes with your Dashboard? Again, the most important element of your Dashboard is that it fits your life as well as your unique working and learning styles.

The weekly check-in that will work best for me is:

_____

_____

_____

I've created recurring calendar events on:

_____

_____

_____

**LEARN MORE ABOUT
CERTIFIED B CORPS**

**LEARN MORE ABOUT
CONSCIOUS CAPITALISM**

**DOWNLOAD TEMPLATES FOR
WEEKLY, MONTHLY, QUARTERLY,
AND ANNUAL REVIEWS HERE**

www.inspiringcowgirl.com/goingfirst

Quarterly Review

Once you've chosen one sphere to focus on each month, set a tentative schedule for revisiting that plan every three months to ensure that the spheres you're focusing on are the timeliest for where you're at that at time and plan for the months ahead.

Your quarterly review is also a perfect time for checking in with your progress and how you're feeling. During each quarterly review, think about your answers to the following questions:

How are you allocating your time, energy, and attention across the entire Dashboard?

What results are those efforts having in the Me, We, and World dimensions?

What pitfalls have you been succumbing to?

What adjustments do you want to make going forward to get more aligned with your purpose?

Annual Review

Whether you choose the first week of January, your birthday, or the end of the year, set aside an hour or so to review your Dashboard from the previous year and envision what you want it to look like in the year to come. Download the Annual Planning Template via the QR code below. to review what went well, what you missed, and what you learned in the past year. Those answers can inform any changes you want to make in terms of starting or stopping activities as well as what you want to keep doing.

My annual review is scheduled for

_____

_____

_____

DOWNLOAD THE ANNUAL PLANNING TEMPLATE

www.inspiringcowgirl.com/goingfirst

Engaging Your Party Guests

No Purpose Party is a success without other people. So when living and evolving your Dashboard, remember to also check in with those you've invited to the party. The Dashboard is most enjoyable and effective when you use it with other people. Whether you share the tool with friends, colleagues, or your social media audience, talking about your impact out loud reinforces your actions. You also model purposeful leadership for the people around you, giving them permission and even inspiration to reflect on their own investments of time and energy. And you create accountability partners for yourself. When people around you hear you talk about your focus on the Self Sphere for this quarter and then see you looking a bit frazzled, they're more likely to ask about that commitment you had shared than comment on your stress out of the blue.

So have a conversation and share your desire to align with your purpose, the questions it's raising for you, and the ways it's making you think about how you *should* behave. Therein lies the power of Going First. By sharing your interest in aligning with a larger purpose, you start to normalize it and make it safe—and eventually a default for those around you to do the same.

To keep me on the path of purposeful leadership, I can share this process with these people:

Even better, would you invite them to a real purpose party, in the form of a Purpose Party Playgroup? To learn more about how to host a Playgroup and get free resources and support, follow this QR code.

LEARN MORE ABOUT HOW TO HOST A PLAYGROUP AND GET FREE RESOURCES AND SUPPORT

www.inspiringcowgirl.com/playgroup